The Politics of
Jacksonian Finance

The Politics of
Jacksonian Finance

JOHN M. McFAUL

Cornell University Press

ITHACA AND LONDON

First published 1972 by Cornell University Press.
Published in the United Kingdom by Cornell University Press Ltd.,
2–4 Brook Street, London W1Y 1AA.

International Standard Book Number 0–8014–0738–9
Library of Congress Catalog Card Number 72–4635

Printed in the United States of America by Kingsport Press, Inc.

Librarians: Library of Congress cataloging information
appears on the last page of the book.

In memory of my father
John Jay McFaul

Contents

Preface

Although much has been written on Jacksonian politics and banking, the political and economic questions about the period have not been resolved up to now. In offering yet another view of banking policy during the Jacksonian era, I do not intend to praise or denigrate the work of previous historians but rather to present new evidence and to characterize the new conclusions drawn from it. First of all, a cursory review of some of the historiography of the Jacksonian period is in order.

Once we were told a simple tale of wealthy bankers, merchants, and planters (the upper classes) supporting Whiggery while the Jacksonian coalition of small farmers and laborers (the lower classes) gave their allegiance and their votes to the Democrats. Arthur M. Schlesinger's *The Age of Jackson,* which depicts an enduring struggle between economic privilege and the forces of egalitarianism, was the culmination of scholarship favorable to Jackson. Schlesinger's conclusions are such an important (and controversial) part of our historiography that his major findings hardly need restatement here.[1]

1. Arthur M. Schlesinger, Jr., *The Age of Jackson* (Boston, 1945). The historiography of the Jacksonian era is discussed most percep-

Reaction to this pro-Jackson scholarship was supplied most impressively by Bray Hammond's *Banks and Politics in America*.[2] Hammond argued that the real impetus for Jacksonian Democracy was the acquisitiveness of the General's supporters, particularly their desire to remove the economic restraints of the Second Bank of the United States, which denied them access to the abundant credit they wanted.

The disagreements between Schlesinger and Hammond exemplified the much-favored dualism between conflict and consensus. In the former view, the Jacksonians were public-minded sentries guarding the government and the public against business domination; in the latter, or consensus view, Jacksonians and Whigs merely disagreed on how best to usher in the Gilded Age. While there has not been much further research on either view, the entrepreneurial-consensus theory has received widespread acceptance throughout the historical profession.[3]

---

tively by Charles G. Sellers, Jr., "Andrew Jackson versus the Historians," *Mississippi Valley Historical Review*, XLIV (March 1958), 615–634; Alfred A. Cave, *Jacksonian Democracy and the Historians* (Gainesville, Fla., 1964); and Edward Pessen, *Jacksonian America: Personality and Politics* (Homewood, Ill., 1969).

2. Bray Hammond, *Banks and Politics in America from the Revolution to the Civil War* (Princeton, 1957).

3. In merging the so-called entrepreneurial and consensus schools of Jacksonian history I am aware that the various historians arbitrarily grouped together here differ somewhat in emphasis and methodology, and perhaps, in some cases, in substantive interpretation. The term is used here and throughout the book to indicate two general historical propositions regarding the Jacksonian era. (1) The apparently substantive conflicts between Jacksonians and their opponents were in reality only conflicts in style and approach and these minimal differences must be placed in the context of a consensus on fundamental beliefs and values. (2) In the field of political response to economic change, Jacksonians and their opponents cannot be polarized as radical versus conservative, anticapitalist versus capitalist, pro-

A part of this acceptance may be attributed to Hammond's skill in translating the complexities of the banking issue into simpler terms. Hammond's experience as a Federal Reserve banker enabled him to cut through the technicalities of bills of exchange, post notes, discounts, and other financial details that bewildered and bored other historians. But more than that, Hammond subordinated these technicalities, and any real conflict over them, to his major persuasion that most Americans—Jacksonians and Whigs alike—hungered for the credit that banks offered. Besides, he argued, the complexities of banking were appreciated at the time by only a few, such as Nicholas Biddle, who vainly tried to moderate the acquisitiveness of Jacksonian Democracy.

The entrepreneurial theory of Jacksonianism coincided with significant stirrings among historians over the use of the behavioral sciences in historical research, especially the techniques of social psychology. Rather than pursue the conflict in the traditional political-economic terms of Schlesinger and Hammond, later historians found it more interesting to probe the Jacksonian mind. Hammond himself provided the idea that the new historical approaches would exploit by suggesting that the Jacksonian anti-banking impulses were two-pronged. First, most Jacksonians wanted more banks and less governmental interference; the language of laissez faire and their hypocritical attack on monopolies were means toward those goals. Secondly, he recognized that a residue of sincere anti-banking mentality did exist (although the emphasis was

---

business versus anti-business, or even pro-banking versus anti-banking. For a recent discussion of the historical literature under review here see Pessen's *Jacksonian America*, ch. 10, and his valuable bibliographical essay, especially the section entitled "The Modern Jacksonian Controversy," 384–393.

upon thought rather than deed)—an attitude he dismissed as quaint and anachronistic in an age of steam and credit.[4]

Post-Hammond historians seized upon this point, rigorously analyzing the Jacksonian anti-banking rhetoric. Psychological probing of the Whigs found them to be looking forward with a keen and realistic eye to an economic bonanza, but Jacksonians, although they shared Whiggish expectations, kept glancing over their shoulders at a fondly remembered and idealized past. Whiggery inevitably won; the Jacksonians, however, reaped the immediate political rewards because of their unconscious ability to articulate the fears, prejudices, and expectations of the masses. In this view, the Old Hero is portrayed as the moralist who eased the guilt feelings of the public by defining its rapacious actions as a disinterested crusade against the aristocratic enemies of the virtuous Republic.

This theory has many attractions, not the least of which is the impressive and imaginative handling of the sources by Marvin Meyers, Louis Hartz, and others.[5] The attribution of rational, calculating economic motives to the Jacksonians by entrepreneurial scholars now seems less valid in light of these studies, and less interesting.

The labors of another discipline, the new economic historians, seem further to minimize the need for any resolution of the diverse findings of Schlesinger and Hammond. By using the techniques of quantification, they have taken the economic problems of the Jacksonian period out of the hands of the relatively unskilled and removed them to a higher level

4. Hammond, *Banks and Politics*, 326–329.

5. Marvin Meyers, *The Jacksonian Persuasion: Politics and Belief* (Stanford, 1957); Louis Hartz, *The Liberal Tradition in America* (New York, 1955); John M. Ward, *Andrew Jackson: Symbol for an Age* (New York, 1955).

of statistical competence. In general, the new economic history has subordinated the influence of American politics upon the era's economic development to the influence of the international economy. To quote the most recent and forceful exponent of this view: "The inflation and crises of the 1830's had their origins in events largely beyond Jackson's control and probably would have taken place whether or not he had acted as he did. The economy was not the victim of Jacksonian politics; Jackson's policies were the victims of economic fluctuations." Disagreements among the new economic historians over sophisticated economic data only support the conclusion that neither the politicians nor the masses in the Jacksonian era were capable of a clear understanding of the economic influences that shaped their lives.[6]

The economic and political conflicts of the era have thus been divided between the two disciplines. Economic analysis is ceded to the econometricians; political analysis is left to the psychological historians, who search the rhetoric of the period for peculiar distortions of reality and their significance. Nevertheless, the recent Jacksonian historiography coming out of both camps shares a common assumption that people are unwitting victims of forces they either do not understand or cannot control.

Perhaps the more traditional historical methodology that portrayed man as the largely rational and conscious molder of

6. Peter Temin, *The Jacksonian Economy* (New York, 1969), 16–17; George Macesich, "Sources of Monetary Disturbances in the U.S., 1834–1835," *Journal of Economic History*, XX (Sept. 1960), 407–434, and "International Trade and United States Economic Development Revisited," *ibid.*, XXI (Sept. 1961), 384–385; Jeffrey G. Williamson, "International Trade and United States Economic Development: 1827–1843," *ibid.*, XXI (Sept. 1961), 372–383; Douglas C. North, *The Economic Growth of the United States, 1790–1860* (Englewood Cliffs, N.J., 1961).

his own destiny should be abandoned. But before relying too heavily upon social psychology and other interdisciplinary methods, we need a firmer resolution of the "old" issue of Jacksonian political-economic intentions. The following study does not propose to diminish the value of these new perspectives. Indeed, it has been influenced and, it is hoped, improved by them. Nonetheless, this analysis has met the Jacksonian society on its own terms and has assumed throughout that the people of that era made political choices as rational, free-willed men.

My research was supported by grants from the California State College at Long Beach, including a semester's leave for further research and rewriting. I also received a summer grant from the American Philosophical Society, for which I am grateful.

Portions of Chapter 3 appear in revised form, by permission, from "The Outcast Insider: Reuben M. Whitney and the Bank War," by Frank Otto Gatell and myself, *Pennsylvania Magazine of History and Biography*, XCI (1967), 115–144.

I owe a great deal to several individuals. My first and most important obligation is to my wife, Evelyn, who has read, corrected, and improved every draft of this manuscript. Among my colleagues who have offered advice I wish to thank Henry Cohen of Loyola University, Chicago, and James Roger Sharp of Syracuse University. Allen Weinstein of Smith College read the entire manuscript thoroughly and perceptively and offered many valuable suggestions. Frank Otto Gatell of the University of California at Los Angeles offered many helpful criticisms and has generously shared with me his knowledge of the Jacksonian era. Finally, Charles Sellers of Berkeley guided the writing of this work in an earlier form. His encouragement, advice, and support have resulted in great profit to me, and I am greatly indebted to him for his impeccable scholarship, unfailing support, and valuable friendship.

JOHN M. McFAUL

Berkeley, California

The Politics of
Jacksonian Finance

1

The Entrepreneurial Myth

From the removal of deposits through the independent treasury proposal Jacksonians labored to develop a banking and fiscal policy that discredits their reputation as advocates of credit expansion and laissez faire. The dismantling of federal controls and the use of state banks as federal depositories were not the culmination of Jacksonian aims. The political positions and legislative actions of the Democrats, distinct from those of the Whigs, offered significant alternatives to the public, though, to be sure, the Whigs and Democrats were not entirely dug into ideological trenches during the banking wars of the 1830's. Although some Jacksonians did defect from White House leadership to join a more cohesive Whig opposition, the Democratic banking policy, as it evolved, moved unswervingly from a vague belief in the desirability of hard money to the advocacy of regulatory powers over banking by public monitors.

The above conclusions depart significantly from the widely held entrepreneurial views of Bray Hammond and others. If it was true that the national Bank limited state bank profits by restricting their note issues (and this was one of the well-publicized arguments in favor of its recharter), then it seems logical that state bankers would support an administration which promised to remove such restraints. The entrepreneurial school has concluded that the banking community was divided between Jacksonians and their state bank allies on one side and the national Bank and its supporters of credit restraints on the other. This is not to imply, of course, that these historians regard this as the only conflict in the Bank War, merely that as far as the politics of banking is concerned the division ran along these lines.

It is not true that state bankers were the natural enemies of a national bank; on the other hand, the relationship between the Bank of the United States (BUS) and the various state banks was not altogether harmonious either. The financial dealings between the national Bank and the state banks were often strained and clumsy, but Biddle was sensitive to the irritations which could arise from such a situation and assiduously courted the interests of his fellow bankers. Initially his efforts paid off in significant and visible pro-Bank support from state bankers. One must resist the temptation to reverse the entrepreneurial conclusion, however, and claim that state bankers were the unqualified supporters of a national bank, for the qualifications are important (as will be shown in a later analysis of the relationship between state banks and the national Bank).[1]

The most important consideration in evaluating the role of state banks during the Bank War and its aftermath revolved around the firm politicizing of the banking issue by Jackson. The overt state bank support for Biddle's Bank declined rapidly after Jackson's re-election; state bankers could figure election returns as readily as they could figure interbank balances. Like their national Bank counterparts, state bankers preferred to operate outside the political sphere because they

1. For a recent analysis of state bank support for the BUS see Jean Wilburn, *Biddle's Bank: The Crucial Years* (New York, 1967).

sensed accurately enough that the outbreak of a bank war could not be contained on the national level but would spread rapidly to the states where brushfire bank wars might become a dominant political theme. In such a situation the odds were high that the "banking interest" would be subordinated to political expediency. After the collapse of the national Bank, the disorganized state bankers moved cautiously and apprehensively. On one hand the promise of financial rewards appealed to their natural cupidity; on the other, the political uncertainty and fiscal turmoil of Jacksonian policy reinforced their hostility. In short, bankers wanted fiscal stability and political neutrality (except when their charters were up for renewal from state legislatures), and in both cases their interests dictated peace on the political front, not a bank war.

There is still a certain plausibility about the entrepreneurial version of Jacksonian Democracy, even if Bray Hammond and others have misjudged the interests and actions of state bankers. The theory's credibility can be traced to two sources. First, historians of various sympathies have found it impossible to accept at face value the rhetoric of the Jacksonians, particularly their self-portrait as disinterested champions of the common man, battling an entrenched aristocracy. One tends to agree with the entrepreneurial historians that more selfish motives were actually at work. Second, after dismissing the rhetoric, we are left with the reality of the national Bank's collapse and the rampant speculation of the 1830's. The entrepreneurial historian has forged the link between the two and thus claims to have properly explained the period's major events and uncovered the real Jacksonian motives.

Bray Hammond has skillfully and thoroughly detailed the actions initiated on both fronts of the Bank War—the White House and the Bank headquarters on Chestnut Street. He has patiently analyzed the executive actions leading to the veto and deposit removal to reveal their entrepreneurial motives, deceptively couched in typical Jacksonian agrarian terms; Biddle's high-minded ineptitude is a testimony to his miscalculation of the public's acquisitive mood, according to Hammond.[2] Entrepreneurial history, therefore, offers a common-sense connection between Jacksonian intentions and subsequent events: the credit expansion and Panic of the 1830's were inevitable by-products of Jacksonian speculative aims.

This causal connection would be more impressive if the evidence for it were not drawn almost exclusively from the period 1829–1833. The entrepreneurial version of Jacksonian Democracy tentatively rests its case after the removal of the deposits to state banks. Hammond virtually ignores the Treasury management of pet banks after deposit removal, but this is not surprising, given the entrepreneurial assumption that the Jacksonians sought the end of financial restraints, not their resumption by the Treasury.[3] Actually, the management of pet banks moved awkwardly toward the assumption of those monetary powers allegedly despised in the national Bank. Many forces shaped this development, among them the administration's recognition that the responsibility for the national economy necessitated some form of fiscal control. The analysis presented here emphasizes Treasury operations

2. Bray Hammond, *Banks and Politics*, chs. 11–14.

3. Hammond discusses the international financial difficulties and Biddle's efforts to shore up the economy preceding the 1837 collapse, then concludes: "During the progress and retrogression of these events, the administration in Washington had been having a pitiful time, starting with the May morning, two months after Mr. Van Buren became President, when his Secretary of the Treasury looked in the newspapers and found that all the banks—even the pets where the government's money was—were refusing to pay out coin" (*ibid.*), 487.

during the pet banks era (1833–1837) and suggests the need for a more comprehensive explanation of Jacksonian banking policy. Again, I do not mean to reverse the entrepreneurial thesis by implying that Jacksonians were the new central bankers of their day; only that Democrats moved in this direction under a variety of economic and political influences which have not been clearly understood.

One of the major topics appearing throughout this work is the tangled relationship between economic change and political response. In this regard I deal with and share many of the same precepts as those held by entrepreneurial and consensus historians. However, one of our basic disagreements concerns the entrepreneurial interpretation of Jacksonian political behavior, especially its assumption that the Jacksonians were so peculiarly representative of the public will (notably its economic aggression) that they encountered little resistance in achieving their political and economic goals. The entrepreneurial historians recognize a political opposition, of course, but explain its lack of effectiveness by the consensus theory. According to this theory, the anti-Jacksonians not only underestimated the popular American consensus, but compounded their misjudgment by accepting the Jacksonian definition of the social conflict and rushing forth to do imaginary battle with the dangerous "radicals."[4]

This study, by contrast, documents the existence during the era of real political differences between Whigs and Democrats—alternatives which were articulated, proposed and

4. This brief summary cannot do justice to the skill and persuasiveness of the entrepreneurial-consensus historians in presenting their major conclusion that the socioeconomic conflicts which coincide with class antagonism are absent from American political behavior. The most forceful exposition of this view is Louis Hartz's *The Liberal Tradition in America* (New York, 1955).

voted on—in other words, measurable political behavior. In measuring this behavior through roll call votes, it is clear that in what were alleged to be important issues dealing with banking and currency, Jacksonians were on one side of the issue in significant numbers while the Whigs and other opposition groups were most often on the other.

These political conflicts remain relatively unexamined because so much recent Jacksonian historiography has concentrated upon the era's rhetoric. It is this analysis of political rhetoric which has buttressed the consensus argument. Most politicians, it is argued, talked in a somewhat different style about the same things; actual political conflicts were minimal and unimportant. But these conflicts require explanation; the consensus interpretation assumes too much and explains too little. The present study, concentrating both on rhetoric and on congressional roll calls, concludes that the rhetoric is significant only when considered along with the political behavior which it helped to determine.

The political analysis throughout this work provides a clearer test of how Democrats and Whigs responded to banking and closely related issues. Perhaps more important, this analysis of congressional behavior makes clear the existence of Jacksonian intraparty divisions which had a critical influence on the development of Democratic banking policy. Jackson's contemporaries and historians alike recognize a division in Democratic ranks between the so-called hard-money agrarian radicals and the pro-business soft-money Jacksonians. But political behavior concerning banking issues cannot be explained as a simple tug of war between these two forces. Many politicians found themselves straddling a line between personal conviction on one side and party doctrine and the public mood on the other. These political variables might shift rapidly, forcing hasty changes in political alignments.

Under certain circumstances congressional Democrats might support hard-money action, not out of ideological preference but simply out of political necessity. The interaction between political rhetoric and the decision-making process on both the executive and congressional levels forms an important part of the analysis to follow.

The independent treasury issue proves malleable to entrepreneurial purposes, receiving considerable attention from Bray Hammond. Hammond portrays the independent treasury proposal as consistent with the Jacksonian preference for laissez faire because, he argues, it further freed state banks from possible governmental regulation. He attributes the political turmoil over the issue to the inability of bankers and their allies to understand that the Jacksonians were actually their friends, not their enemies. Bankers, believing the Jacksonians when they declared the independent treasury proposal to be an anti-bank measure, opposed what was really in their best interest. Once again the entrepreneurial-consensus version of the period offers misunderstood rhetoric to explain what otherwise would appear to be a divisive political issue.[5]

The issue of the independent treasury, as it is handled here, is shown to be a part of the political-economic turmoil immediately preceding the Van Buren proposal; furthermore, it is argued that the proposal as submitted to Congress by the Van Buren administration was consistent with the patchwork of economic and political compromises worked out by the Treasury in the pet banking experiment. Rather than proposing that state banks be freed from further regulation, as entrepreneurial historians maintain, the bill submitted to

5. Hammond, *Banks and Politics*, 496–499; for a recent, detailed analysis of the struggle over the independent treasury see James C. Curtis, *The Fox at Bay: Martin Van Buren and the Presidency, 1837–1841* (Lexington, Ky., 1970), chs. 4–7.

Congress contained provisions which would have allowed stricter regulations than the expedient measures implemented by the secretary of the Treasury during the pet banks era. The regulatory provisions were clearly understood by both advocates and opponents of governmental bank regulation; it was precisely this understanding, rather than any misunderstood rhetoric about the proposal, which accounts for much of the political conflict surrounding it.

The anti-bank rhetoric that Jacksonians had employed so successfully since the war on the "Monster" Bank paved the way for acceptance of the independent treasury proposal, which was to be a remedy for the economic collapse of 1837; the same rhetoric, however, defeated the administration's original goal for the further regulation of state banks. Throughout the thirties Jacksonians had portrayed themselves as the natural enemies of banks, but they were not unanimously agreed on a strategy toward that enemy. Some Jacksonians argued that banks should be kept at arm's length while others felt an obligation to tame the abuses of banking in the public interest. The ultimate position of the first group was legal and political separation of banks and the state; the second argued for state regulatory powers over banking. Such diversified positions are not new to American politics and therefore not surprising; what is interesting is the degree to which the Jacksonians managed to adhere to both positions, thus implementing Treasury regulation of banks while preaching the virtues of political separation from all banks. This unstable compound which had served Jacksonians during the pet banks era finally separated into its distinct parts during the struggle over the passage of the independent treasury. When it became necessary to choose btween the alternatives of regulation and laissez faire, the rhetoric of separation proved more persuasive than the argument for the advantages of retaining political connections with state banks.

As a consequence of the strategy of separation, the administration's plan for continuing state bank regulation through the independent treasury by allowing governmental acceptance of bank notes for rapid redemption was scrapped by Congress in favor of a plan which required the government to receive only specie. The latter promised an end to political responsibility for banking and was widely heralded as being a stronger anti-bank measure. Under the circumstances, Jacksonians found it impossible to resist such a solution and the Democratic party, after a short-lived and troublesome flirtation with bank regulation, abandoned that responsibility to those Wall Street interests that the Jacksonians had been accused of favoring in the first place.

In summary, some of the more important differences between the findings of this study and those of the entrepreneurial-consensus school of Jacksonian history are noted briefly. The economic interests and political actions of state bankers have been misinterpreted by entrepreneurial historians. The amount of support for a national bank within the state banking community has been overlooked, and the degree of fiscal conservatism which pervaded banking circles, especially in the larger eastern cities, has been underestimated. Entrepreneurial historians ignore the significant (if not always successful) Jacksonian attempts to regulate the pet banks through administrative edict and congressional legislation after deposit removal. Their interpretation of political behavior during the era is generally challenged throughout this study, which emphasizes, rather than consensus and insignificant opposition, the existence of meaningful political divisions between Jacksonians and the opposition, as well as important political conflicts within the Jacksonian coalition. On the latter point, the way in which intraparty compromise influenced political decisions regarding banking policy has not been appreciated previously.

Finally, the general entrepreneurial conclusion that the accomplishments of Jacksonian politics were the triumph of laissez-faire principles is seriously questioned here. The Jacksonian attraction to laissez-faire rhetoric is undeniable; nor is any attempt made to evaluate the degree to which Jacksonians implemented laissez-faire policies in areas other than banking. But it will be shown that throughout the banking conflict the Jacksonians were neither unqualified preachers nor enthusiastic practitioners of laissez-faire principles. On the basis of these conclusions, the entrepreneurial thesis, as it applies to Jacksonian Democracy, requires severe modification if not abandonment.[6]

Does this analysis of Democratic banking policy then advocate a return to Schlesinger's class conflict thesis? While this study tends toward that analysis, attempts have been made throughout to indicate where and how it differs. Some general disagreements can be summarized here. Arthur Schlesinger imposes upon Jacksonian political behavior a rational, purposeful, ideological pattern made up of the contradictory forces of anti-bank, hard-money interests drawn from the class-conscious eastern cities and the pro-inflation Democrats from western America. This ideological confusion was re-

6. I am not implying that pet banking has been neglected entirely or that the entrepreneurial conclusions have received unqualified acceptance. For recent studies which chip away at the entrepreneurial monolith see Charles Sellers, *James K. Polk, Jacksonian* (Princeton, 1957); Harry N. Scheiber, "The Pet Banks in Jacksonian Politics and Finance, 1833–1841," *Journal of Economic History*, XXIII (June 1963), 196–214; Frank Otto Gatell, "Sober Second Thoughts on Van Buren, The Albany Regency and the Wall Street Conspiracy," *Journal of American History*, LIII (June 1966), 19–40; Robert V. Remini, *Andrew Jackson and the Bank War* (New York, 1967). The most impressive and sophisticated treatment of early American banking is Fritz Redlich, *The Molding of American Banking: Men and Ideas* (2 vols.; New York, 1947, 1951).

solved, so he argues, after the Bank War when the real hard-money purposes of the Jacksonian program were gradually revealed, and the soft-money western Jacksonians were either forced aside or bit their lips and remained loyal to the Old Hero for personal reasons.

Jacksonian banking policy was the result of neither an ideological timetable of entrepreneurial designs nor radical, hard-money purposes. When Democratic actions seem to display either tendency, more often than not the reason can be traced to some temporary political expediency. Schlesinger's point that hard money became increasingly important to Jacksonian policy after 1833 is accepted in this analysis but attributed to political necessity rather than ideological commitment.

The destruction of the BUS created a number of economic and political problems neither foreseen nor initially understood by Jacksonians. Of paramount importance was the necessity for renewed purpose and political justification following the climactic Bank War; hard-money rhetoric filled this need. The repeated invocation of the virtues of hard money satisfied many Jacksonians that they were continuing the battle on a new front. It was further employed to justify the apparent unnatural alliance between the Jackson administration and the pet banks. In this dilemma the Jacksonians found themselves in a situation similar to that of the Jeffersonians, whom they claimed to admire greatly. In order to govern effectively, specifically to manage the unwieldy pet banking structure, the Jacksonians were forced to abandon their laissez-faire prescription as a remedy for all political ailments. In doing so they simply argued that cooperation between the government and private banks was necessary to achieve the Golden Age of increased specie circulation. The emphasis upon specie gave the Treasury potential leverage for managing banks through Treasury-imposed specie requirements against bank liabilities. Because it could unite Jacksonians of such politically diverse views as those opposing all banks and those recognizing the necessity for regulation of banks, hard money became the distinctive rhetorical property of the Jacksonians following the Bank War.

One of the most recent and illuminating studies of Jacksonian politics is Richard McCormick's *The Second American Party System.*[7] McCormick concludes that nonideological variables were paramount in determining political behavior under the second party system. He cites as primary causal forces the contest for the presidency and the regional consequences of such a contest, the balance or lack of it between contesting parties in determining the degree of voter participation, and the legal, constitutional changes that occurred. In emphasizing political structure rather than social conflict, McCormick supplies a much needed corrective to those who might minimize the constitutional, legal apparatus in American politics.

McCormick's statistical findings are sober reminders of the hazards of accepting too readily the participants' own descriptions of the issues at stake and how the electorate responded to those issues. He demonstrates, for example, that the greatest degree of voter participation did not occur in the elections that leading politicians of the time defined as critical referendums on issues of the greatest importance.[8] Still, the present work concludes that it would be a mistake to overlook the influence of issues on Jacksonian politics. Admittedly the organizations, mechanisms, and forms of political action were

7. Richard P. McCormick, *The Second American Party System: Party Formation in the Jacksonian Era* (Chapel Hill, N.C., 1966).

8. See especially McCormick's "New Perspectives on Jacksonian Politics," *American Historical Review,* LXV (Jan. 1960), 288–301.

important, perhaps decisive, in implementing democratic politics; but once formed the political structure required vitality
and rhetorical justification. It was not enough for politicians
to point to the Herculean political structure which held up
the American republic; they also felt they must moralize the
necessity for such elaborate efforts in the first place. For this
purpose, issues like the Bank and hard money were critical in
defining political boundaries. This analysis concludes that the
Jacksonian hard-money rhetoric had a considerable influence
on the decision-making process of the 1830's.

Organized political parties were still unacceptable to a
number of citizens of that day, branded as "factions" by some
and probably viewed suspiciously by most. Above all, political parties lacked authority and legitimacy; nor had they yet
proven any high degree of effectiveness to endear them to
most Americans on practical, nonideological grounds.[9] In
responding to the new egalitarian politics, which required
new organizations and techniques, the superior talents of the
Jacksonians have been noted frequently. They are portrayed
as superb organizers, businesslike about political life, quick
to recognize and exploit political opportunities, and perhaps
temperamentally a bit more enthusiastic and comfortable
with the altered political circumstances than their opponents.
Once organized, the Jacksonians proved themselves superior
with weapons of political rhetoric. They assumed the banner
of the "people's" party, labeling the opposition as the "aristocrats," and generally flattered and pleased the voting public.

The use of political rhetoric by the Jacksonians, whether
sincere or demagogic, was politically rewarding. An influential analysis of Jacksonian rhetoric is given in Marvin Meyers'

9. For a recent analysis of this theme see Richard Hofstader, *The
Idea of a Party System: The Rise of Legitimate Opposition in the
United States, 1780–1840* (Berkeley, Calif., 1969).

The Jacksonian Persuasion. Meyers finds that the Jacksonian political language stirred deeply engrained American beliefs in convincing the public of the paradoxical argument that although cherished values were threatened by a changing world, the Jacksonians would restore the virtuous republic without restricting those economic pursuits which would make such restoration impossible.[10] As challenging as this thesis is, it assumes that Jacksonian rhetoric served merely to persuade other politicians and the electorate that they were pursuing some morally redemptive course, when the evidence shows that Jacksonians not only talked differently from their opponents about banks and hard money, they acted in politically different ways. The Jacksonians not only talked about hard money, they voted for it; nor did they merely denounce banks from the platform, they voted against bank interests when the issue was presented in those terms. Whigs and pro-bank Democrats were convinced that Jacksonians were opposed to banks and the economic activities they represented, and they reached this conclusion by examining the same kind of evidence presented here—the votes of Jacksonian politicians. This is not inconsistent with Marvin Meyers' thesis that the Jacksonians employed a peculiar rhetoric, but the emphasis in the present study is upon the fact that Jacksonian political language, whatever other purposes it served, did indeed influence Jacksonian political action.

This study, then, documents a curious but at the same time familiar pattern of events in American political history: it demonstrates that Jacksonians with their anti-state, anti-government bias ended up strengthening both state and government. It shows how fragile is political ideology in American politics, especially when that ideology conflicts

10. See especially the provocative discussion by Meyers in *The Jacksonian Persuasion*, chs. 2, 6.

with political actions necessary to govern effectively. Furthermore, it supports the argument that political organizations are important as a causal force but concludes also that the political rhetoric which reflects basic values and beliefs often shapes and determines the course taken by the political organizations. In other words, politicians often literally talk themselves into certain kinds of political action.

2

The Monsters in Conflict? State Banks and the Bank of the United States

The assumption that Jackson's attack on the BUS received the enthusiastic support of state banks is an important part of the thesis that Jacksonian Democracy represented aggressive business interests chafing under BUS restraints. The most widely shared grievance, the entrepreneurial thesis maintains, was the national Bank's restrictive regulation of state bank-supplied credit. Two other factors forged the alleged anti-BUS alliance between state banks and the administration. Some state institutions coveted the federal deposits for their own banks; powerful financial interests along the Eastern seaboard, especially in New York, wanted to replace the Philadelphia "Monster" as the national Bank headquarters. These narrow, selfish interests are symbolic to many historians of a national mood of expectant capitalism during the Jacksonian era—a mood which demanded the relaxation or abandonment of credit restrictions, a more democratized use of the public money, and a "friendlier" national bank.

Both opponents and supporters of the national Bank courted state bank support. The unresolved issue is not whether state banks recognized that their interests were involved in the

Bank War but rather what actions those interests dictated. Even though state bank cupidity is an important part of the entrepreneurial thesis concerning the Bank War, evidence of widespread state bank support for the administration is not part of that interpretation. Frank Blair, aided principally by Amos Kendall and Reuben Whitney, came to Washington to develop a national political strategy based partly upon state bank hostility to the BUS. Blair repeatedly argued in Washington *Globe* editorials that state banks *should* support the administration, and the *should* has become *did* in many historical accounts.[1]

The logic of the Blair-Kendall plan was based upon the faulty assumption that the BUS contraction after the Panic of 1819 would help to enlist state banks in the administration's projected attack upon the Bank more than a decade later. Though it is true that some wounds heal slowly, financial grudges are too costly to be held by institutions for long periods. Biddle's astute management of the BUS after 1823 avoided collisions between the national and state banks. He knew the sentiments and interests of state bankers throughout the country and expected their support in any conflict with Washington Jacksonians.

The most visible sign of state bank involvement in the Bank War occurred during the early months of 1832, when the issue was BUS recharter. In January, Biddle confidently instructed his branch bank managers to urge local state banks to petition Congress in favor of recharter.[2] Politically, this course was not without peril. Favorable petitions could be dismissed by Jacksonians as proof of BUS domination of state institutions; furthermore, banks were hardly popular political

1. Washington *Globe*, Jan. 19, April 27, 30, 1831.
2. See Nicholas Biddle's letters for Jan. 16, 1832, Nicholas Biddle Papers, Library of Congress.

allies. But Biddle reasoned that such action was necessary to disprove the Jacksonian allegation that his institution was hostile to state banks and therefore a flagrant example of irresponsible national power.[3]

State bankers from all sections of the country responded to Biddle's appeal. This support for the national Bank from among its alleged foes will be described and analyzed state by state, dividing the country into the regional categories of South, West, Middle Atlantic states, and New England.

In Mississippi there were only two state banks in existence during the recharter struggle. The Bank of the State of Mississippi was in the process of going out of business; its place was to be taken by the Planters Bank, chartered in 1830. Both banks petitioned Congress in favor of BUS recharter.[4]

The State of Louisiana had five banks in 1832 and three of them, representing more than half the state's banking capital, petitioned Congress for BUS recharter. Between 1832 and 1836, however, ten new banks were chartered in Louisiana, including the two New Orleans banks which became the administration's pets in November, 1833.[5]

Alabama had only two banks, the Bank of Mobile, a small-capital bank chartered during territorial days, and the Bank

3. "What we wish is to disarm the opponents of the Bank of their great weapon—the supposed jealousy of the State institutions" (Biddle to Isaac Lawrence, Jan. 23, 1832, *ibid*).

4. Jean A. Wilburn, *Biddle's Bank: The Crucial Years* (New York, 1967), 35; J. Van Fenstermaker, *The Development of American Commercial Banking: 1782–1837* (Kent, Ohio, 1965), 152; *House Journal*, 22 Cong., 1 sess., 510.

5. Van Fenstermaker, *American Commercial Banking*, 128–129. The petitioning Louisiana banks were the New Orleans Canal and Banking Company, Bank of Orleans, and the Louisiana State Bank (*Senate Documents*, 22 Cong., 1 sess., no. 108; *House Journal*, 22 Cong., 1 sess., 534, 450). The two pets were the Union Bank of Louisiana (1832) and the Commercial Bank (1833) (*Senate Documents*, 23 Cong., 2 sess., no. 13).

of the State of Alabama. Both were reported to favor re-charter, but the Bank of the State of Alabama, which monopolized the state's banking activities, remained discreetly neutral in public, while the less important Bank of Mobile petitioned for recharter.[6]

None of the fifteen state banks in Georgia petitioned Congress. Nor did BUS recharter receive any open support from the six South Carolina state banks. North Carolina had three state banks, and two of them, representing three-fourths of the state's banking capital, petitioned Congress for recharter.

Virginia, the last and most populous southern state to be considered, had four state banks. Only one, the small-capital Northwestern Bank of Virginia in Wheeling, petitioned Congress in favor of BUS recharter.[7]

The South had fewer state banks than either the Middle or New England states. By January 1832, the southern states had thirty-seven chartered state banks in operation, approximately eight per cent of the nation's total number.[8] Of these, only nine petitioned Congress for BUS recharter. However, taking account of the response by states makes the region appear more pro-BUS: all Mississippi's banks sent petitions as did more than half the Louisiana and North Carolina banks; only the Georgia banks were known to be decidedly unfriendly to the national Bank.[9]

6. Van Fenstermaker, *American Commercial Banking*, 112; Wilburn, *Biddle's Bank*, 40; *Senate Journal*, 22 Cong., 1 sess., 143.

7. Van Fenstermaker, *American Commercial Banking*, 119, 165, 183; Wilburn, *Biddle's Bank*, 40–43; *House Journal*, 22 Cong., 1 sess., 474, 385; *Executive Documents*, 22 Cong., 1 sess., no. 167.

8. These figures are compiled from Van Fenstermaker, *American Commercial Banking*, Appendix A.

9. The Wilburn study presents the petitions by states without reference to the total number of state banks. This arrangement leads the author to conclude that a "heavy majority" of the region's banks

Other factors add to the conclusion that southern state banking interests were more pro-Bank than the meager response of nine out of the region's thirty-seven banks seems to reveal. With few exceptions, all the state banks which petitioned Congress were large-capital, commercial banks. Furthermore, the hub of southern commercial development was New Orleans: significantly, three out of the five New Orleans banks petitioned Congress for BUS recharter, including the $4 million New Orleans Canal and Banking Company. At this juncture the administration had failed to win the allegiance of important New Orleans bankers in its struggle with the national Bank.

Failure to petition Congress did not in itself indicate state bank hostility toward the national Bank, however. The Bank of Cape Fear in North Carolina did not petition Congress in favor of BUS recharter but did refuse the government deposits after removal; this means that all three of the state banks in North Carolina opposed Jackson's policies. Federal deposits were handled in North Carolina by a bank chartered after the BUS veto, which was also the case with New Orleans pet banking.[10] In South Carolina there were five large-capital banks located in Charleston and one small-capital bank in Columbia during the recharter struggle. None of them petitioned Congress, but all five Charleston banks subsequently refused the government deposits.[11]

Finally, the response, or lack of it, from Virginia state

---

were pro-BUS (Wilburn, *Biddle's Bank*, 44–45). This may be a legitimate conclusion but not from the evidence Wilburn presents.

10. *Senate Documents*, 25 Cong., 3 sess., no. 304. The government's North Carolina pet was the Bank of the State of North Carolina, chartered in 1833 and selected by the Treasury in April 1835 (*Senate Documents*, 23 Cong., 2 sess., no. 13).

11. *Senate Documents*, 25 Cong., 3 sess., no. 304.

banks is significant in any analysis of the relationship between state banks and the national Bank. The four banks in Virginia included two large-capital Richmond banks, the Bank of Virginia (presided over by faithful Democrat John Brockenbrough) and the Farmers Bank of Virginia, and two small-capital banks in the western part of the state. Virginia state banking was characterized by multi-branch operations based upon interbank deposits. The result was a conservatively managed state system which maintained Virginia Bank notes at par throughout the state.[12] The absence of support for the BUS within important banking-political circles in both Virginia and New York is directly related to the establishment within each state of a banking system which its advocates believed minimized excessive note issues while it maximzed opportunity for responsible commercial expansion. Accordingly, the national Bank was regarded as a regulative competitor by the New York Safety Fund champions and the conservative financial overlords of Virginia state banking.[13]

The one Virginia state bank which petitioned Congress for BUS recharter was the small-captial, Northwestern Bank at Wheeling. Because of its isolation in the western part of the state, it was the only Virginia state bank whose notes circulated at a discount.[14] The Northwestern Bank fits the stereotype of "wildcat" bank operation but responded to the Bank War in uncharacteristic fashion. Although the BUS imposed regulation on all banking activities, the aggressive Bank of Virginia with its sprawling branches was threatening to

12. Van Fenstermaker, *American Commercial Banking*, 183–184.

13. On New York, see the Annual Report of the Bank Commissioners for 1830 in *Assembly Documents*, I, no. 59. Virginian confidence in state banking regulation is reflected in Documents 23 and 26 of the *Journal of the House of Delegates* for 1834.

14. Van Fenstermaker, *American Commercial Banking*, 84.

anachronize the fledgling Northwestern Bank and force it out of business or into financial impotence. Fearing the direct competition from and possible absorption by their more powerful neighboring banks more than it feared the national Bank, the Northwestern Bank chose the neutral financial stewardship of the BUS over the threat of encroachment by powerful state systems. The Virginia experience supports the conclusion that different state banking situations dictated different responses to the administration's Bank War.[15]

The West, with the exception of Ohio, was virtually without state banks during the recharter struggle. The financial havoc following the Panic of 1819 closed down banking activities throughout the western region and the BUS efficiently filled the economic vacuum with the help of Ohio state banks.[16] Approximately seventeen chartered state banks existed in Ohio and four of them petitioned Congress for BUS recharter. The four Ohio banks each had capitals of $500,000, the highest capitalization allowed Ohio state banks. The most significant pro-BUS petition came from the Commercial Bank of Cincinnati, the only bank in this center of western commerce besides a branch of the BUS. The Commercial Bank was allowed to double its capital—to $1,000,000—in 1833, and was chosen a government pet the next year. Actually, it had not considered the national Bank an obstacle to its financial success. The national Bank provided valuable banking captial for Cincinnati and the entire western area, and the direct result of the withdrawal of BUS operation would be

15. Gatell, "Sober Second Thoughts on Van Buren," *Journal of American History*, LIII (1966), 40.

16. Van Fenstermaker, *American Commercial Banking*, 90–91; Wilburn, *Biddle's Bank*, ch. 5. The West includes the states of Ohio, Tennessee, Kentucky, Indiana, Illinois, and Missouri.

the chartering of numerous state institutions which would vainly try to replace the credit and services previously provided. The officers of the Commercial Bank of Cincinnati recognized this competitive threat. Their BUS support was motivated by self-interest and a desire for economic expansion of the western area.[17]

State banks in the Middle Atlantic states held a larger percentage of banking capital (approximately 37 per cent) than those of any other region of the country, although New England had a greater number of banks.[18] The number of Middle Atlantic state banks which petitioned Congress for BUS recharter was only twenty-five out of one hundred and forty state-chartered banks. But if the responses are analyzed by state and consideration is given to the size and location of banks which sent petitions, the twenty-five responses reveal significant pro-Bank sentiment among the region's important state bankers.

Delaware had four state banks, only two of which were fairly large. There were $500,000 captial banks in the cities of Wilmington and Dover. Delaware having no BUS branch, the Dover bank had been employed by the Treasury since 1820 to handle the small amount of government transactions within the state; such employment perhaps restrained the Dover bank from sending any petition for BUS recharter. The large capital bank in Wilmington did petition Congress

17. The four were the Bank of Chillicothe, Commercial Bank of Cincinnati, Belmont Bank, and the Farmers and Mechanics Bank of Steubenville (*House Journal*, 22 Cong., 1 sess., 225, 408, 413, 474; Van Fenstermaker, *American Commercial Banking*, 166–167; *Senate Documents*, 23 Cong., 2 sess., no. 13; Wilburn, *Biddle's Bank*, 48).

18. Van Fenstermaker, *American Commercial Banking*, 77, 80, 111. The Middle Atlantic region includes Delaware, New Jersey, Maryland, Pennsylvania, and New York.

in favor of BUS recharter and was joined by the small-capital Bank of Smyrna.[19]

New Jersey had twenty state banks: three petitioned Congress in favor of BUS recharter. However, most of the state's banks were small-capital institutions, some capitalized as low as $50,000. Only three New Jersey banks were capitalized above a half million; one of these, the State Bank at Camden, did respond in favor of BUS recharter, joined by the Trenton Banking Company and the Cumberland Bank at Bridgetown which together represented another one-half million of the state's banking capital.[20]

Four of the fifteen Maryland state banks responded to Biddle's call for support. However, more important than the statewide response was the manner in which Baltimore banking interests responded, since the city dominated banking operations throughout the state. All four of the pro-Bank petitions came from Baltimore banks. These represented one-half of the city's eight banks as well as one-half of Baltimore's banking capital.[21]

Pennsylvania banks responded strongly to the recharter struggle in favor of the national Bank. Fifteen of the state's thirty-five banks sent pro-Bank memorials to Congress. Again, it was the large-captial, more commercial and most significant state banks which came to the defense of the national Bank. The financial center of Philadelphia consisted of nine banks with $12 million in banking capital (excluding the BUS). Seven of these nine institutions, representing $10 million of

19. *Ibid.*, 115; *Executive Documents*, 23 Cong., 2 sess., no. 27; *House Journal*, 22 Cong., 1 sess., 186; *Senate Journal*, 22 Cong., 1 sess., 154.
20. *House Journal*, 22 Cong., 1 sess., 444, 257–258, 510.
21. The four Baltimore banks were the Mechanics Bank of Baltimore, The Bank of Baltimore, Commercial and Farmers Bank, and the Franklin Bank (*ibid.*, 385, 413, 444, 510).

the city's banking capital, petitioned Congress in favor of BUS recharter.[22]

New York state banks, in contrast to Pennsylvania institutions, offered almost no support to Biddle in his struggle with the Washington Jacksonians. Only the small-capital New York State bank in Albany sent a petition in favor of BUS recharter.[23] But silence on the part of New York state bankers should not be interpreted as long standing hostility to the national Bank. The apparent stability provided by the state's Safety Fund operations minimized state banking appreciation of the regulatory functions of the BUS. More important in evaluating the response of New York bankers is an understanding of how rapidly the bank issue was politicized in New York; Van Buren and other Jacksonians regarded the state's ratification of Washington policy as crucial.[24]

New England state banking operations differed from those in either the West or the South. Instead of a few banks in each state with extensive state involvement, there were numerous small-captial banks. The tax structure in most New England states made it advantageous to charter new banks rather than to increase the capital of existing ones. Despite the large number of banks, New England banking was managed in a conservative fashion. The concentration of specie in the area and the Suffolk bank system helped to maintain

22. The seven Philadelphia banks were the Bank of Pennsylvania, Farmers and Mechanics Bank, Philadelphia Bank, Bank of Pennsylvania Township, Bank of Northern Liberties, Commercial Bank of Pennsylvania, and Bank of North America (*ibid.*, 212, 225, 286, 330, 412). The eight outside Philadelphia were the Farmers Bank of Bucks County, Bank of Pittsburgh, Kensington Bank, Bank of Germantown, Bank of Chester County, Bank of Montgomery County, Bank of Chambersburg, and Monangahela Bank (*ibid.*, 258, 286, 385, 412, 413).

23. *Ibid.*, 413.

24. Gatell, "Sober Second Thoughts on Van Buren," *Journal of American History*, LIII (1966).

the high quality of bank notes throughout New England.[25]

The relative financial maturity of New England minimized the urgency in those states of the BUS recharter. Only twenty-three of their more than two hundred state banks petitioned Congress. There was no state bank response from either Rhode Island or Maine, only two favorable petitions from Connecticut, and four from Massachusetts. Vermont and New Hampshire banks gave the strongest support from the New England states. Seven of Vermont's thirteen banks petitioned Congress as did ten of New Hampshire's twenty-one.[26]

In general, Biddle must have been pleased with the state bank response to his call for public support. The total numbers of state banks which either petitioned or did not petition Congress is not overly significant in itself. If it were, one would have to conclude that the Administration had no state bank support, since no state bank petitioned Congress against BUS recharter. But it is misleading to discuss state banks as though they were all alike. Banks varied greatly in the business interests they served, in the degree and type of public control to which they were subject, and in their capital and correspondent relationships with other banks. Furthermore, as indicated, differing state financial systems, or the lack of

25. Van Fenstermaker, *American Commercial Banking*, 77–80.
26. The two Connecticut banks were the Thames Bank and the Norwich Bank (*House Journal*, 22 Cong., 1 sess., 474). The four Massachusetts banks were the Grafton Bank, Bunker Hill Bank, Concord Bank, and Lowell Bank (*ibid.*, 436, 899). The seven Vermont banks were the banks of Rutland, Vergennes, Burlington, St. Albans, Caledonia, Orange County, and Bank of Windsor (*ibid.*, 330, 444, 510). The ten New Hampshire banks were the Exeter Bank, Union Bank, Rockingham Bank, Bank of New Hampshire, Piscataqua Bank, Winnipiseogee Bank, Stafford Bank, Dover Bank, Bank of Lebanon, and Farmers Bank of Amherst (*ibid.*, 286, 293, 330, 385, 413, 444; *Executive Documents*, 22 Cong., 1 sess., no. 110).

them, and the political situation within each state significantly influenced state bank responses to the BUS recharter issue.

The attitudes of state bankers towards BUS recharter may be divided into three loose groupings. Some state bankers were relatively indifferent, especially those associated with the small-capital New England banks. This indifference may be directly related to the fact that the services of the BUS were not as critical to this area as they were to other regions of the country.[27] A second attitude was that found among bankers operating within relatively efficient state regulatory systems like those of Virginia and New York. These bankers were for the most part cautiously hostile to BUS operations. Their opposition stemmed from their belief that the national Bank needlessly and perhaps arrogantly exercised monetary functions that their banks already provided on the state level. Therefore, the quarrel was not over central banking so much as whether these powers should be exercised through state and regional arrangements or be imposed by a national institution.[28]

27. The celebrated Henshaw proposal for a new national bank argued that the BUS withdrawal would not hurt New England. The national Bank's capital in New England represented a small part of the region's total banking capital; furthermore, he argued that New England bank notes circulated at par without BUS regulation (*Senate Documents*, 22 Cong., 1 sess., no. 37).

28. The Bank of Virginia was a state replica of national bank operations. Brockenbrough played the role of financial statesman by repeatedly warning the legislature against excessive banking and note issues. A Bank of Virginia director suggested to the legislature that the bank be strengthened "to exercise a salutary control over the other banks within the State." A select committee on banking in the 1834 legislature praised regional and state systems of bank regulation such as the Suffolk and Safety Fund Systems and recommended a "well regulated system of mother banks with branches" for Virginia rather than many independent banks (*Journal of the House of Delegates, 1834*, Document nos. 23 and 26). For New York, see the

A third response to BUS recharter among state bankers was unqualified support. It came primarily from large-capital institutions in such commercial centers as New Orleans, Cincinnati, Baltimore and Philadelphia. This response could be characterized as typical of the conservative, responsible banks as opposed to the more aggressive, less responsible institutions eager to capitalize on the national Bank's removal. However, the most vocal pro-BUS support came from the Southwest and West, those areas of the country where the most speculative economic growth would take place.[29] The typical western entrepreneur of the 1830's, eager to capitalize on lands, crops, cotton and slaves, did not look upon the national Bank as an obstacle to those goals but rather as a means of attaining them.

State banking interests probably had less influence on the recharter issue than either Biddle or Blair had hoped. But Jackson's decision to remove the federal deposits from the Bank in the fall of 1833 necessitated direct state bank support and widespread acceptance in the financial community. It might be assumed that the natural cupidity of state banks to increase their profits through the use of the federal funds would dictate their allegiance to administration policy. But the removal of federal funds from the Bank did not mean that all state institutions would share the financial windfall. Actually, the administration was faced with a difficult task in reconciling state bankers to the deposit removal decision. It was necessary to find responsible banks in the commercial areas

---

Annual Report of the Bank Commissioners for 1830 in *Assembly Documents*, vol. I, no. 59. The Henshaw proposal also boasted that the Safety Fund system made New York State banks "as sound and secure as any in the world" (*Senate Documents*, 22 Cong., 1 sess., no. 37).

29. Wilburn emphasized the strong BUS support from these areas (*Biddle's Bank*, ch. 5).

of the country (where pro-Bank sentiment was strongest) and keep the number of Treasury agents limited for administrative efficiency and financial security, while convincing the rest of the banking community that such a system would not mean an end to the liberal credit and regulatory services formerly supplied by the BUS and its branches.

The administration's most pressing problem was finding state banks in the large eastern cities which would agree to accept the federal funds and provide the services required by the Treasury. The public controversy preceding removal produced some favorable inquiries from state banks, but hardly enough to insure that a sufficient number of reliable banks would serve the Treasury. Kendall's excursion in the summer of 1833 to sound out the banks along the eastern seaboard was undertaken to put down the many doubts raised in Washington regarding the willingness and abilities of state banks to handle Treasury responsibilities.[30]

Kendall and the administration succeeded in enlisting the services of enough state banks to begin a nationwide pet banking system, not because state banks were eager to destroy the national Bank and get the public money for themselves, but rather because Jackson's resolution to terminate the national Bank made the governmental use of some state banks inevitable. The disintegration within the banking community which resulted from the removal policy necessarily motivated each bank to maximize its own particular advantage. If a bank in Philadelphia, New York City, or Boston were to refuse the public money, another bank could be found to take the funds; even if all the banks in a given city were to refuse the deposits they would go to a sister city, thereby increasing

30. Gatell disputes the thesis that state banks were reluctant to receive the federal deposits ("Spoils of the Bank War," *American Historical Review*, LXX [1964], esp. n. 8).

the banking capital in a rival metropolis.[31] The administration took advantage of the dilemma facing the banking community and hastily erected a twenty-four bank system of pet banks to handle the federal finances. Privately, Treasury secretary Roger B. Taney assured state bankers that the pet bank system would be as advantageous as the former national Bank with its branches; in public, the Jacksonians proclaimed noisily and rather nervously that they had proven the national Bank unnecessary.

Nicholas Biddle and the supporters of a national bank rallied their forces for a counterattack on Washington policy; the BUS chief was convinced that one of his strongest weapons in the fight would be an increase of the already considerable pro-Bank sentiment among state bankers. Pro-Jackson historians have portrayed Biddle's BUS management following deposit removal as a reckless, irresponsible gamble to force Congress to restore the federal funds and recharter the Bank. Such statements by Biddle as the following to Congressman John Watmough serve as partial documentation for this thesis: "My own course is decided—all the other Banks and all the merchants may break, but the Bank of the United States shall not break."[32] Pro-Bank historians justify Biddle's policies as financially sound or at least understandable, given govern-

31. For example, Albert Gallatin, hardly a BUS foe, solicited the Treasury for the appointment of his New York City National Bank as a government pet once the deposit issue was settled (Gallatin to Taney, Sept. 26, 1833, Letters from Banks, United States Treasury Papers, National Archives). The Bank of Louisiana applied for the deposits to prevent the federal funds from going to a bank in Cincinnati (A. Thurston to Taney, Feb. 17, 1834, *ibid*).

32. Biddle to Watmough, Feb. 8, 1834, in Reginald C. McGrane, ed., *The Correspondence of Nicholas Biddle Dealing with National Affairs, 1807–1844* (Boston, 1919), 221; Arthur M. Schlesinger, Jr., *The Age of Jackson* (Boston, 1945), 103.

mental hostility. It is not my intention here to reopen the debate on this point, but rather to demonstrate how Biddle's strategy after removal was designed to intensify the financial problems caused by the disruption of the relationship between state banks and the national Bank. Biddle's plan for a well regulated system of national finance, directed by disinterested public servants, was threatened by what he considered demagogic, irresponsible, self-seeking politicians; only by experiencing the financial chaos he knew would follow the demise of this system would the public realize the dangerous consequences of Jacksonian folly.

Biddle was not quite, however, the financial bully of Jacksonian imagination. While no one has credited Biddle with political acumen, he was keenly aware of the necessity for discretion in using the Bank's financial power to sway Congress. He knew that a severe BUS contraction would turn important financial interests as well as the public sharply against the Bank, especially when Jacksonians would interpret every hostile move as a validation of the "Monster's" irresponsible use of power. By gradually reducing BUS loans he could turn the financial screw without bearing down too hard and still be solicitous of state bank interests wherever possible. The BUS president would not stand by and let state banks "break." (Biddle reserved these flamboyant statements for convincing Washington congressmen that only a vote against Treasury policy would bring relief.) The BUS President understood state bankers' interests, realizing that they grudgingly accepted the necessity for regulation and appreciated the functions of bankers' bank supplied by his institution. Biddle's strategy was designed to convince state bankers of the contrast between the intelligent guidance and sympathetic generosity of the BUS and the political uncertainties and financial absurdities of Washington policy. Although his plan failed politically, it was nonetheless based upon the sound assumption that state banks identified their own interests with those of the national Bank.[33]

The response of state banks, pet and non-pet, to removal and the financial stringency which followed that action adds credence to Biddle's conclusion that state banks tended to support a national bank. But this tendency had to be discreetly expressed because of the political atmosphere surrounding the bank issue. While a new deluge of pro-Bank, anti-removal memorials did descend upon the Congress which convened in December 1833, few came from state banks and only banks from four states sent them: Connecticut, Maryland, New Jersey and Pennsylvania.

Five Connecticut banks petitioned Congress to restore the deposits and recharter the national Bank. Actually this was an increase over the previous winter when only two Connecticut banks had sent pro-Bank petitions. The same two small-capital Norwich banks again responded favorably to the BUS cause, but this time were joined by three of the state's largest banks located in Hartford: the Hartford Bank, the Phoenix Bank, and the Connecticut River and Banking Company. The motivation of the three Hartford banks is easily explained. Besides the three already mentioned banks in Hartford, there was a fourth, the Farmers and Mechanics Bank, chartered in May 1833. Six months after receiving its charter, the Farmers and Mechanics Bank was chosen as a government pet. Charges of political favoritism, which surrounded this choice, only added to the suspicion and rivalry of the other Hartford banks toward the newly appointed government pet.[34]

33. Govan, *Nicholas Biddle*, 244–259; Bray Hammond, *Banks and Politics*, 438–442.

34. *Senate Documents*, 23 Cong., 1 sess., no. 459; Gatell, "Spoils of the Bank War," *American Historical Review*, LXX (1964), 53–54.

Four Maryland banks petitioned Congress in March 1834 to restore the deposits and recharter the Bank. It was the same number which had been in favor of recharter the preceding winter, but the petitions did not come from the same banks. In the preceding Congress, when recharter was the issue, the BUS had received the support of four of the eight large-capital Baltimore banks. But by the spring of 1834, Jackson's veto and removal policy had significantly altered financial and political reality. Democrats were lining up House support for the administration's actions. Baltimore being a Democratic stronghold,[35] its bankers, whatever their inclinations, would be understandably cautious about taking a public stand against the administration at this crucial time. Furthermore, part of the federal funds were deposited with a Baltimore pet, the Union Bank of Maryland.

The four Maryland banks which petitioned Congress during the "panic" session were the three small-capital banks in Frederick and a newly chartered small-capital bank in Williamsport. Their actions may have been politically motivated, hoping to aid the Whig cause by their petitions, but it is more likely that the petitions reflected intrastate conflicts. The political pattern in Maryland was often determined by the struggle between Baltimore and the rest of the state; the development of Maryland banking conformed to this pattern. The fact that the state's banking capital was concentrated in Baltimore resulted in banking demands from other areas of the state, especially from the hinterland and potential rivals to the Baltimore port. The Farmers Bank of Maryland (whose Frederick branch petitioned Congress) was chartered in 1805

---

35. Richard P. McCormick, *The Second American Party System: Party Formation in the Jacksonian Era* (Chapel Hill, N.C., 1966), 163–164.

to aid the agricultural hinterland, and its headquarters in Annapolis created a potential competitor to Baltimore.[36]

Maryland returned to an orthodox banking course after the Panic of 1819. There was a need for an expansion of banking capital in Maryland and the national Bank seemed the likeliest source of credit expansion. But the administration's removal of deposits and use of one Baltimore bank promised little in the way of credit resources for the rest of the state, and would be considered by non-Baltimore banking interests as support for that city's long-standing hegemony over the state's economy. Furthermore, Baltimore appeared more interested in developing its trade with the Pennsylvania hinterland than with the Maryland interior.[37] Consequently, small-capital banks in the Maryland interior preferred the relatively disinterested BUS guidance to Washington policy which promoted Baltimore at the expense of the rest of the state.

Three New Jersey banks petitioned Congress to restore the deposits. Two of them had petitioned Congress during the recharter struggle: the state bank at Camden and the Cumberland Bank at Bridgetown. This time they were joined by the Camden branch of the Farmers Bank of New Jersey. The two Camden banks probably identified their interests more with Philadelphia than with New Jersey. The state bank at Camden centered its business at its Philadelphia agency, since there were only a thousand people in Camden.[38]

36. *Senate Documents*, 23 Cong., 1 sess., nos. 194, 459; McCormick, *Second American Party System*, 163; Alfred C. Bryan, "History of State Banking in Maryland," *Johns Hopkins University Studies in Historical and Political Science*, XVII (1899), 23.

37. Jane N. Garrett, "Philadelphia and Baltimore, 1790–1840: A study of Intra-Regional Unity," *Maryland Historical Magazine*, LV (1960), 1–13.

38. *Senate Documents*, 23 Cong., 1 sess., no. 459; Bruce H. French, *Banking and Insurance in New Jersey: A History* (Princeton, 1965), 27.

Pennsylvania state banks again offered the strongest BUS support. Twelve Philadelphia banks petitioned Congress during the "panic" session, including three banks chartered in 1832. The Philadelphia banks were joined by four more outside the city, two from Pittsburgh, one from Lancaster, and a fourth from Chambersburg.[39] These responses from the Pennsylvania banking community could be dismissed by Jacksonians as the actions of financial puppets under the control of the "Monster," but it seems more reasonable to conclude that Pennsylvania bankers were acutely aware of the value of the BUS and that their responses reflected this as well as state pride in being the home of the national Bank.

Some explanation is required, however, for the fact that fewer state banks responded to the removal issue than to that of recharter. If it is true that state banks strongly supported a national bank, why did they fail to support the BUS at such a crucial time in its life? One explanation might be that state bankers had only belatedly become aware of the benefits of Treasury policy and were silently awaiting the financial rewards, either directly, through appointment as government pets, or indirectly, through a general expansion of state bank credit. But state bankers were not unintelligent about their own interests and the fact is that, except for the lingering hope that Jackson might consent to a new national bank, the governmental use of state banks was expected from the time that BUS recharter became an issue. Consider the case of the

39. The twelve Philadelphia banks were the Bank of North America, Bank of Pennsylvania, Farmers and Mechanics Bank, Commercial Bank of Pennsylvania, Bank of Germantown, Schuylkill Bank, Mechanics Bank, Bank of Pennsylvania Township, Manufactures and Mechanics Bank, Moyamensing Bank, Western Bank of Philadelphia, Philadelphia Bank (*Senate Documents*, 23 Cong., 1 sess., nos. 20, 459). The four non-Philadelphia banks were the Bank of Pittsburgh, Merchants and Manufacturers Bank of Pittsburgh, Farmers Bank of Lancaster, and the Bank of Chambersburg (*ibid.*, no. 459).

Bank of Pittsburgh: A small-capital bank in the western area of the state, it obviously hoped to grow and expand with the area it served. The institution's growth came in 1834 when it was allowed to triple its capital, from $400,000 to $1.2 million,[40] and yet the Bank of Pittsburgh petitioned Congress both to recharter the national Bank and to restore the federal deposits. Obviously, this bank did not believe that its interests would be furthered by the destruction of the national Bank. Of course, it can be argued that the bank's directors did not know that they would be allowed a capital increase after the BUS withdrawal, and that therefore no connection exists between the two events. But historians have repeatedly pointed to this alleged connection in explaining state bank hostility to the national Bank, that is, that the former expected to profit at the withdrawal of the latter. Obviously the directors of the Bank of Pittsburgh did not perceive such an eventuality and felt that the interests of the institution over which they presided were furthered by the continuance of a national Bank.

The decline in public state bank support for the BUS in the post-removal period is better explained by Jackson's forceful politicizing of the Bank issue. Now that the president had committed himself and the Democratic party on the issue of a national bank, public statements on this issue were watched carefully for their political significance. Bankers might disclaim political interests but were very much aware of the reprisals and rewards from political action on both the state and national level. A political blunder by a bank's directorate raised the possibility of counterattack by Democratic state legislators and financial neglect from the Treasury at Washington. These may have been remote possibilities, but bankers are known for their cautious ways; their interests in the after-

---

40. Van Fenstermaker, *American Commercial Banking*, 171.

math of the Bank War dictated a noncombatant position and a public posture of neutrality.

Behind the public facade of neutrality, however, even among pet bankers there were some who left no doubt about their dissatisfaction with the pet banking system. The Bank of Louisville gave up the deposits in February 1834; the financially powerful and politically important Bank of Virginia had rescinded its contract with the government the month before.[41] The administration's system could survive a few defectors but Taney was having difficulties with his most trusted pets. The success of the pet bank system depended to a great extent upon its operations in the large eastern cities, where two of Taney's staunchest pet banks seemed to be working hand in glove with the department: the Union Bank in Baltimore and the Philadelphia Girard Bank.

The Union Bank's economic problems began immediately after appointment as a pet bank. Its president, Thomas Ellicott, used the government deposits for speculative ventures. Taney felt betrayed and acutely embarrassed because of his personal connections with the bank. Unfortunately for the Treasury, the Union Bank's durability became a test of the pet bank system. Taney realized the symbolic as well as financial importance of pet banking in Baltimore and grimly continued to give Treasury support to the beleagured Union Bank. Ellicott, for his part, took advantage of Taney's position to pressure the secretary for even more financial aid. Biddle's advice to the Union Bank was to give up the deposits as the first step out of its difficulties.[42]

41. A. Thurston to Taney, Feb. 17, 1834, Letters from Banks; Richmond *Enquirer*, Jan. 7, 1834.

42. Thomas Ellicott to Taney, March 14, 1834, David Perine Papers, Maryland Historical Society; Taney to Ellicott, March 25, April 15, 18, 1834, Taney Papers, Library of Congress; Biddle to Webster, May 28, 1834, Biddle to Reverdy Johnson, June 2, 1834,

Ellicott also recommended such a couse in late May in an interview with Taney, but the secretary lectured Ellicott about their "struggle for the liberties of the country" and encouraged the Union Bank to hold on—with Treasury support, of course. Taney later complained of Ellicott's "cool, calculating duplicity with which he has been tormenting me for his own private gain."[43] Biddle's intervention in Baltimore banking during this crisis period was dramatic and swift, and calculated to remind bankers of the advantages of a national bank. The BUS president rushed specie to his Baltimore branch for emergency aid to local banks; the Union Bank, he advised to turn to the government for support.[44]

The Philadelphia Girard Bank was being pressured to join other Philadelphia banks in demanding a restoration of the deposits and BUS recharter. William Lewis, the cashier, made a hurried trip to Washington in February 1834 to see Jackson personally about the bank's difficulties. The trip increased rumors that the bank was about to cancel its government contract. The bank's directors met that month and voted eight to three in favor of retaining the deposits, but agreed to call a general stockholders' meeting within thirty days to reconsider the matter.[45]

Biddle Papers. The tangled relationship between Ellicott, Baltimore financial interests, and the Washington Treasury is analyzed in Frank Otto Gatell's "Secretary Taney and the Baltimore Pets," *Business History Review*, XXXIX (1965), 205–227.

43. Taney to Ellicott, May 23, 1834, Taney Papers; Taney to Perine, July 2, 1834, J. C. Oliver Papers, Maryland Historical Society.

44. R. Colt to Biddle, April 14, 15, 17, 1834, Biddle Papers. Biddle had predicted to John C. White, his Baltimore branch bank manager, a few months after removal that state banks would "regret the absence of so forbearing a creditor as the Bank of the U.S. has been" (Biddle to White, Nov. 10, 1833, J. C. White Papers, Maryland Historical Society).

45. Philadelphia *Pennsylvanian*, Feb. 14, 20, 1834.

The unpredictability of government calls on the pet banks aided those who argued that the government deposits increased a bank's instability. This argument seemed to gain strength when Reuben Whitney (by this time an unofficial pet banks coordinator) warned Lewis that the government would have to make heavy drafts on his bank throughout the month of March. Advocates for retaining the deposits used the familiar argument of intercity rivalry, predicting that the deposits, once surrendered, would go to New York City to further increase her financial prominence.[46]

Stockholders holding the largest blocks of stock in the Girard Bank were strongly in favor of returning the deposits. They called a strategy meeting a week before the scheduled general meeting to devise means for forcing the bank to give up the deposits, and asked Biddle for his advice. These stockholders demanded that the bank's directors follow their wishes rather than those of the majority of the stockholders. Upon hearing this, Whitney began to worry about the effect of wealth upon the republic: "My individual opinion is, that a majority of stockholders should govern, not of stock. If the weight of wealth is to preponderate, in our Government and institutions, what does it lead to?" What it led to in this case was the annulment of the contract between the government and the bank and its refusal to receive further deposits, in accordance with the wishes of its largest stockholders.[47]

The Bank of Virginia gave up its pet bank status in January of 1834. John Brockenbrough, its president, worked with

46. Whitney to Lewis, Jan. 22, 1834, Lewis Neilson Papers; *Pennsylvanian*, March 2, 8, 1834.

47. A. Henry to Biddle, March 28, 1834, Biddle Papers; Whitney to Lewis, March 20, 1834, Lewis Neilson Papers; James Schott to Taney, April 21, 1834; Lewis to Taney, June 2, 1834, Letters from Banks.

Virginia politicians and other bankers to pressure the administration to restore the deposits. Both Brockenbrough and the Richmond *Enquirer's* Thomas Ritchie, in April of 1834, suggested to Andrew Stevenson, the Virginia Democrat and House Speaker, that Jackson renew the deposits in the national Bank. The *Enquirer* had already hinted that there was a difference between restoring and renewing the deposits, and Brockenbrough assured Stevenson that such a plan would at least "baffle the designs" of the opposition in Congress.[48]

Of course, financial necessity can make strange political bedfellows. Pet bankers during the winter of 1833–1834 may have been scurrying to save their institutions from the folly of their own shortsightedness in attacking the Bank in the first place. For a banker, a reversal of policy is a wiser choice than political fidelity to a financially hazardous cause.

Such an explanation might well fit the case of John Brockenbrough, who believed that a system similar to the Virginia state system of branch banking, with its easy redemption and financial conservatism, could be employed nationwide through a network of state banks. The point is that the Virginia Bank president was opposed to the national Bank but not to bank regulation. He knew at first hand the problems as well as the benefits of imposing credit restrictions and complained about his own branches resisting the regulation he imposed from the "mother" bank in Richmond. After the collapse of pet banking in 1837, Brockenbrough pointed to the lack of any "concerting principle" among state banks and "the jealousies and rivalries between them" that caused their experiment with the Treasury to fail. Brockenbrough attrib-

48. Richmond *Enquirer*, Jan. 9, 1834; J. Brockenbrough to A. Stevenson, April 26, 1834, Andrew Stevenson Papers, Library of Congress.

uted this failure to fact that state banks are "institutions which consider their own profits so much more than they do the public interests of the country."[49]

His own stewardship of the Bank of Virginia documents his analysis. He accepted pet bank status for his bank in October 1833, surrendered the deposits during the "panic" winter of 1833–1834, and then resumed pet banking operations in Virginia after the Treasury and the administration had weathered the political-financial crisis following removal (the Philadelphia Girard Bank was also reappointed a pet). The fact that Brockenbrough and other state bankers, pet and non-pet, moved to maximize their own profits does not confirm their long-standing or enthusiastic support of Jackson's Bank War. It does, however, tend to bear out Brockenbrough's assessment that the greatest liability of the governmental use of state banks was that inevitably each bank would seek only its own interest. This liability was widely recognized and constituted one of the strongest arguments for a national bank. Thomas Rutherford, a Bank of Virginia director, wrote to the state legislature after the state bank system had been operating for a year: "For the purpose of acting as a restraint on the operations of the state banks generally, I have always regarded the United States bank as a salutary institution." John Grieg, president of the New York upstate Ontario Bank, agreed with him. Writing to another New York state banker in March 1834, Grieg stated that "no permanent relief is to be expected, nor is the prosperity of the Country to be restored, unless the Bank of the United States is allowed to con-

49. Brockenbrough to Woodbury, May 3, 1837, Woodbury Papers, Library of Congress; Brockenbrough to W. C. Rives, May 20, Aug. 5, 1837, William C. Rives Papers, Library of Congress.

tinue its operations by a renewal of its charter or a new national bank equally efficient be incorporated."[50]

If the state banks chosen as deposit banks had not at first realized that their interests were more closely identified with the national Bank than with the Democratic administration in Washington, they did as soon as the administration's monetary reforms were revealed. Bankers were scarcely receptive to the Treasury plan of restricting bank notes of small denomination, since they considered them an important source of profit. The Bank of the United States had been fully aware of state bank interests on this issue. Samuel Jaudon, Biddle's chief cashier, objected to a Senate bill for the recharter of the national Bank during the 1833–1834 Congressional session, not because of the provisions involving the Philadelphia Bank but because of the restrictions on state bank note issues. The Senate proposal called for the elimination of state notes under $20. "This if confined to the Bank of the United States," Jaudon wrote to Biddle, "so as to give the State Banks the whole of the smaller circulation, might and would make friends of them; but to attempt to induce them in such a prohibition is impolitic and I think unwise."[51] Sentiments such as these, contrasting so sharply with the actions and rhetoric of the Democrats, undoubtedly caused some state bankers who had not already done so to question the relative merits of exchanging the sympathetic guidance of the national Bank for troublesome prospects of governmental interference.

Testimony both from supporters and opponents of the administration bear out Biddle's prediction that the disruption of national finance by Washington Jacksonians would rally

50. *Journal of the House of Delegates, 1834,* Document 23; J. Grieg to A. B. Johnson, March 17, 1834, in Albert Bryan Johnson, *Autobiography* (Berkeley, Calif.), 31–32.

51. S. Jaudon to Biddle, March 9, 1834, Biddle Papers.

state bankers to the BUS cause. Senator Daniel Webster, in the "panic" session debate, declared: "Is it not notorious that, with the exception of those banks which have been made deposit banks, the general and prevailing desire of well-conducted state institutions is, that the deposits should be restored and the Bank of the United States continued?" The flaw in Webster's statement is his exclusion of pet banks from the list of BUS supporters. Hezekiah Niles, hardly a BUS sycophant, argued in May 1834: "The Bank has a mighty power. . . . The state banks stand in the relation of rival to it, being engaged in the same business; but where is the state bank that asks the abolition of a bank of the United States?" And Reuben Whitney, looking back on this period a few months later, wrote that the Pennsylvania banks had acted "as if their existence was identified with that of the United States Bank."[52] Nicholas Biddle could smile; personal satisfaction (but not political success) was his. There is no better illustration of the political impotence of the banking interest during the Jacksonian era than its failure to reverse Democratic policy regarding a national bank.

Finally, historical accounts which stress state bank hostility toward the BUS assume a degree of economic ignorance and irresponsibility on the part of state bankers that is not logical. More than any other group state bankers were sensitive to the dangers of an unregulated banking system. Taking into account their own interests as well as some degree of responsibility they assumed for the general economy, it is unreasonable to presume that they would welcome an economic environment of laissez faire. Furthermore, state bankers realized that BUS withdrawal would require an expansion of state banking, creating competition for existing banks. To assume that

52. *Reg. Deb.*, 23 Cong., 1 sess., 437–438; *Niles Register*, May 10, 1834; Whitney to Lewis, Nov. 6, 1834, Lewis Neilson Papers.

they would deliberately encourage increased competition is to assume that state bankers were woefully ignorant of their own interests. Whatever rivalry existed between BUS branches and state banks was more often one of isolated incident rather than a general pattern. Weaknesses in the national Bank system, due in part to the great number of branches and to the lack of efficient communication between them and Philadelphia, sometimes resulted in the BUS branches becoming the "captives" of the local interests they served.[53] There is ample evidence that state bankers preferred such a relationship with BUS branches to having them replaced by numerous directly competitive institutions.

Further evidence of widespread support for some type of central banking during this period is provided by an analysis of the various movements to establish a new national bank. Fritz Redlich has divided central banking advocates of this time into three groups: one favored the BUS, another desired a new national bank, and the third preferred some sort of government bank.[54] Many of Jackson's more cautious supporters hoped that his hostility was directed against *the* Bank rather than *a* bank, as the issue was commonly stated. Therefore, the expectation that Democrats might sponsor a proposal for another national bank divided the advocates of central banking politically and aided the administration's war on the BUS.

One of the more widely publicized national bank proposals originated with David Henshaw, the Massachusetts banker-Democrat. He wrote privately that his proposal was not intended to refute Jackson's constitutional objections, "but if a bank is to be, then we ask to have our claims considered." It

53. Hammond, *Banks and Politics*, 256, 312–313.
54. Fritz Redlich, *The Molding of American Banking: Men and Ideas* (2 vols.; New York, 1947, 1951), II, 179–180.

is no accident that the Henshaw proposal coincided with the BUS recharter application. As he wrote to Edwin Croswell, influential editor of the Albany *Argus, "The effect of this movement I hope will be salutary."* The Henshaw national bank plan has been described as a flagrant example of Jacksonian avarice. But the emphasis upon economic motives obscures the political strategy involved in the timing of the petition to Congress. Henshaw's proposal, along with others, counterbalanced Jackson's Bank veto message, convincing the financially and politically timid that a new national bank would grow out of the aftermath of the Bank War. No one would portray David Henshaw and some other Jacksonians as disinterested public servants, but they were clever politicians and the deliberate publicizing of their memorials to Congress is the key to their strategy. Henshaw and others could have avoided the charge of personal interest by suspending proposals for a substitute national bank until after the 1832 election (unless, of course, the proponents of a national bank were too strong a group to risk alienating). While Jackson and Van Buren did not lend support to the many rumors that a new national bank would be chartered, it is significant that they did not publicly disavow them until after Jackson's re-election.[55]

No section of the country offered stronger testimony of widespread support for a national bank than the West. The sparsely settled, credit-hungry western states depended upon the extensive resources and services of the national Bank to a greater degree than more highly developed areas of the country. Jackson's campaign against the Bank was watched anx-

55. *Senate Documents,* 22 Cong., 1 sess., no. 37; Henshaw to Edwin Croswell, Jan. 23, 1832, Nathaniel Tallmadge Papers, microfilm, Wisconsin Historical Society; Hammond, *Banks and Politics,* 408–409; Govan, *Nicholas Biddle,* 175.

iously by western Democrats, and their letters to Jackson and Van Buren do not support the theory that there was a western uprising against the "Monster."

Warden Pope, a Louisville Jacksonian, warned the president during the summer of 1831 about the *Globe*'s anti-Bank editorials. "Unless a substitute be offered, nine-tenths of the West, will support the present Bank with all its defects. Those who think differently do not know the sentiments of the people. If we go against the present Bank, nothing will save us but a substitute."[56]

From Cincinnati William Hatch advised the vice-president in the summer of 1833 that the people of Ohio were on principle opposed to BUS recharter, but added, "Yet there are many who with cause believe that a National Bank is of great importance to this vast region." The Cincinnati *Republican*, a pro-administration paper, offered to publish a plan for a new national bank as a "feeler" without prominent Democrats having to take a stand on the issue. This would "retain friends and bring in others who hold that a National Bank is . . . important to the prosperity of the West." Hatch lectured the New Yorker on the economic consequences of the Bank War for the West. "On becoming acquainted with the people of the West, understanding their trade, intercourse and circumstances, you will at one glance see the vast difference that exist in regard to this subject, between them, and the residents of states east of the mountains. Along the line of the seaboard exists a succession of cities, possessing an abundance of Bank capital, and all within 48 hours travel." The West did not have adequate state bank capital, and he warned Van Buren that westerners "are well informed in regard to all that con-

56. Warden Pope to Jackson, June 19, 1831; Bassett, *Correspondence of Jackson,* IV, 299.

cerns their own interests." The West supported the veto and Jackson, he concluded, but felt certain that the administration would propose a new national bank. It is important to note that William Hatch, after his pleas for a national bank, advised Van Buren that he was about to become the cashier of the Commercial Bank of Cincinnati. He was well informed about the western economy and saw no conflict between state and national banking interests in that area.[57]

With the removal of deposits to state banks, supposedly a boon to the inflationary banking areas of the South and West, western pressures on the administration for a national bank increased. Moses Dawson, an early Jackson-Van Buren man in Ohio, advised James K. Polk in February 1834 that "superficial friends" were leaving the party over the removal issue, but somberly added: "Indeed there is no little dissatisfaction with some of our true friends arising from apprehension that if the Bank be put down and no substitute raised in its place there may be considerable difficulties occur to our Commercial interests."[58] Staunch administration supporters nervously watched their western allies, suspicious of their fidelity to the Jacksonian cause. Indeed, the Bank War had already taken its toll among the western Jacksonians in Congress.

The two Democratic senators from Indiana, John Tipton and William Hendricks, voted for BUS recharter in the twenty-second session of Congress, as did Democratic Senator John Robinson of Illinois.[59] In the next Congress a Connecticut Democrat claimed that support for BUS recharter

57. W. Hatch to Van Buren, July 22, 1833, Van Buren Papers. The directors of the Commercial Bank shared this view and had petitioned Congress for BUS recharter (*House Journal*, 22 Cong., 1 sess., 408).

58. M. Dawson to Polk, Feb. 17, 1834, Polk Papers.

59. *Senate Journal*, 22 Cong., 1 sess., 345–346.

came not from the businessmen and merchants of the East but from their counterparts in the South and West who depended heavily upon a national bank. "Too many of those from the South and West are in the market," he wrote to Gideon Welles, as an explanation for pro-Bank sentiment within Democratic ranks.[60] The West was "in the market" and hoped to stay there, but many western Democrats obviously believed that western prosperity depended upon the continuance of a national bank: "Without a U.S. Bank, I fear we cannot go on," was the dire prediction of one of Jackson's Cincinnati correspondents.[61] Under these circumstances, the belief or hope that Democrats would charter a new national bank was an important political asset to western Jacksonians.

The most significant and serious proposals for a new national bank came not from the West, however, but from the Empire State of New York where there were complex interactions between politics and the state's banking system. New York state bankers were not a monolithic, economic-political interest group pursuing common goals; the state's banking interests were more often divided than united. An important conflict existed between large-capital New York City banks and numerous small-capital "country" banks in the interior. City banks extended credit through deposit creation and balances left with other banks, relying less upon note issue, while the country banks primarily depended upon note issue as a source of profit.[62] Beside different functions, other con-

60. W. Ellis to G. Welles, March 11, 1834, Gideon Welles Papers, Library of Congress.

61. Jesse Hunt to Jackson, Dec. 26, 1832, Jackson Papers.

62. "The volume of business in New York City was too large to be transacted by the clumsy method of cash payments, and the size and prestige of the banks made their checks acceptable to merchants. In these respects New York was of course far ahead of the rest of the country, and the country banks, although showing the same trend,

siderations divided city and county bankers, notably the Safety Fund Act, designed primarily to insure the banknote holder against loss. The act seemed to place state power behind the small-capital, note-issuing country banks, especially since the state assessed contributions to the Safety Fund upon a bank's capital. The large-capital, city banks objected strenuously on the grounds that they were being unfairly taxed to guarantee the financial practices of country banks.[63]

New York country bank interests resented outside control of their note issues by a national bank, not because they objected to regulation per se, but because they felt that restraints already were being maintained through safety fund legislation. Enthusiasm for the safety fund's effectiveness led influential upstate Democratic banking interests to challenge the national Bank. The state bank commissioners, appointed under safety fund legislation, attacked BUS control over local banks in their 1830 report to the legislature. They argued that competition among local banks in returning each others' notes and the safety fund restrictions were sufficient safeguards of the public interest.[64]

But New York City financiers were neither enthusiastic about the Safety Fund Act nor primarily interested in the note issue functions of banks. The withdrawal of BUS credit from New York City, however, posed a threat to the city's extensive commercial transactions. Jackson's Bank War did not solidify New York State bankers but further divided the

were always more concerned with note circulation than the city banks" (Margaret G. Myers, *The New York Money Market* [New York, 1931], vol. I: *Origins and Development*, 89).

63. Robert Chaddock, *The Safety Fund*, 268–269; Hammond, *Banks and Politics*, 557–558.

64. Annual Report of the Bank Commissioners in New York, *Assembly Documents, 1831*, vol. I, no. 59.

city and country banks. Proposals for a substitute, large-capital, national bank therefore originated in New York City but received little support from upstate Albany Regency Democrats. Regency bank interests were not eager to promote New York City at the expense of fast-growing Albany and establish into the bargain another outside regulator of their bank notes.[65]

The new bank proposals from New York City were often wrongly assumed by the public to have statewide banking support. Nicholas Biddle recognized the advantages of publicizing connections between the administration's Bank War and the self-interests of New York. "The New York Scheme is a curious compound of money and politics," he angrily wrote to George McDuffie upon publication of one of the New York new bank proposals. "It is in fact a project of solemn league and covenant between Washington and Albany."[66] But Biddle's explanation plays fast and loose with the state's geography—Albany is not New York City—and his assumption ignores the different financial interests of city and country banks just described. Biddle was correct, however, in identifying Albany as the source of New York Democratic influence upon Washington policy. Leading New York Democrats such as Van Buren, United States Senator Silas Wright, and Benjamin F. Butler drew political strength from upstate, and to the degree that this political strength was

65. Professor Gatell clearly shows the division within the New York Democracy between the countryside and New York City Democrats. City legislators did not support the Regency-inspired anti-BUS resolutions in the state legislature. Regency suspicions of the New York City Democracy were aided by Albany's economic expansion and jealousy of the city's economic power ("Sober Second Thoughts on Van Buren, The Albany Regency, and the Wall Street Conspiracy," *Journal of American History,* LIII [1966], 31–33).

66. Biddle to G. McDuffie, July 10, 1833, Biddle Papers.

measured in economic terms, New York Democratic influence was closer to the financial interest of note-issuing country banks. Happily, the financial interests of these country bankers coincided with the neo-Jeffersonian policies and presidential ambitions of Van Buren, since both were opposed to national institutions.[67]

Wall Street proposals for a new national bank were adamantly opposed by Van Buren. Writing from New York City shortly after Jackson's re-election in 1832, Van Buren advised the President that "interested men are already caballing in this City to get up a new scheme and if your opinions are allowed to rest in doubt many of our friends will be tempted by their avarice and others by sincere convictions to set on foot applications and measures which can only serve to throw discredit upon the struggle through which we have passed." He then restated his interpretation of the administration's position: "The idea of the establishment of *any bank in any of the States,* is, I take it, entirely done away with by the veto." He urged Jackson to avow these convictions freely in conversations with others. The Albany *Argus,* the Regency press, declared it "impossible" that New York Democrats would support a national bank in New York City after opposing the Philadelphia institution. The Washington *Globe* published an "authorized" statement to the effect that the president would never consent to the charter of a new national bank in any of the states.[68]

The national bank issue was resolved within Democratic ranks; but the financial panic during the winter of 1833–1834 increased the pressure, particularly in New York, for some

67. Cf. Gatell's treatment in "Sober Second Thoughts," *Journal of American History,* LIII (1966).

68. Van Buren to Jackson, Nov. 18, 1832, Van Buren Papers; Albany *Argus,* Jan. 28, 1834; Washington *Globe,* Feb. 11, 1834.

dramatic solution. Van Buren was encouraged by fellow Regency Democrats to support a financial remedy which did not carry the political embarrassment of a national bank and would aid rather than hinder the state's country bank interests. A new state bank was proposed, capitalized at $10 million, called the Bank of the State of New York. The state was to subscribe to one-fourth of the capital, the banks of the seven state senatorial districts were to become one-sixth owners, and the remainder was to be taken by individuals. The bank was expected to replace the capital stock of the BUS branches, handle specie transactions with Europe, and provide depository and creditor functions for country banks. The new state bank "would correspond in the Bank machinery of this State to the balance wheel in the machinery of mechanics," Gideon Lee informed Van Buren.[69] This proposed bank, meshed by its operations and transactions into the state's city-country financial relationship appealed to New York Democrats and promised greater benefits to country bank interests than would a new national bank in New York City.

The value of a large financial institution to the operations of New York country banks was vividly demonstrated by the results of the BUS financial contraction during the winter of 1833–1834. A state bank commissioner advised Van Buren that Albany banks were forced to refuse the paper of interior banks through lack of capital. Thomas Olcott of the Albany Mechanics and Farmers bank called upon another upstate banker, Alexander B. Johnson, for financial aid in preventing a run on two other country banks. Another of Van Buren's correspondents informed him of the growing distress among upstate institutions, stating that the Albany banks had been sustained by $300,000 from city banks. Under such circum-

69. Gideon Lee to Van Buren, Jan. 6, 1834, Van Buren Papers.

stances, the correspondent continued, "The project of a 10 million Bank is a favourite with, I believe all your friends in New York." Thomas Olcott solicited support from other country bankers. Prosper Wetmore, Governor Marcy's close friend, was instrumental in drafting the charter and also planned to play an influential role in the direction of the bank. The chartering of a $10 million state bank rapidly became an important objective of New York Democratic banking interests.[70]

The Regency bank proposal lacked only Van Buren's support, but the Vice-President opposed the plan. Van Buren was concerned about the political consequences of such an action on the part of New York Democrats. The bank's large capitalization and the timing of the proposal, coinciding as it did with the demise of the BUS, was sure to magnify suspicion about New York's position in the Bank War and about Van Buren's role in the attack on the Philadelphia institution. He therefore encouraged his Regency allies to withdraw their support for the state bank plan and fretted in a letter to his son that Biddle was looking for evidence that the deposits had been removed to "promote the views and subserve the interest of New York."[71]

In opposing these New York bank projects, Van Buren was acting in accordance with his commitment to Jacksonianism. The base of his political support was the historic Jeffersonian-Republican alliance between New York and Virginia. The strict-constructionist doctrines of the old Republi-

70. C. Stebbins to Van Buren, March 1, 1834, *ibid.;* Thomas Olcott to A. B. Johnson, A. B. Johnson, *Autobiography,* 25–26; M. Van Schaick to Van Buren, March 12, 1834, Van Buren Papers; Olcott to Johnson, March 15, 1834, Johnson, *Autobiography,* 27–28; Albany *Argus,* Oct. 14, 1836.

71. Van Buren to John Van Buren, Feb. 10, 1834, Van Buren Papers.

can-Jeffersonian school had undergone severe modifications during the heyday of economic nationalism after the War of 1812. But since the collapse of the postwar boom in 1819, the belief that the national government should not aid particular economic interests had renewed appeal. Van Buren's adherence to this neo-Jeffersonian position was fixed before he knew Jackson's thoughts on matters of public policy, as his uneasy letter to James Hamilton shortly after the 1828 election shows: "I hope the General will not find it necessary to avow any opinion upon Constitutional questions at war with the doctrines of the Jefferson school."[72]

The Vice-President's fidelity to Jeffersonian principles would have been called into serious question if the Bank War were interpreted solely as a financial struggle between New York and Philadelphia. His stern letters to fellow New Yorkers, denouncing their plans for a New York bank, were designed to insure that the constancy of his Jeffersonian position remain above reproach.

Van Buren became increasingly sensitive to any public ambiguity over his political creed.[73] To support any national bank proposal now, he wrote to Thomas Suffern, would violate his publicly stated principles, "which I feel it to be a sacred duty to maintain inviolate."[74] Van Buren intended to keep his compact with the people by maintaining his personal integrity and disinterested political behavior. His hope, which

72. Van Buren to J. Hamilton, undated, in James A. Hamilton, *Reminiscences*, 94.

73. Cf. Bray Hammond: "It is vain of course to look for an open avowal of Mr. Van Buren's purpose. He seldom committed himself and then only in terms as equivocal and disarming as possible" (*Banks and Politics*, 354).

74. Van Buren to Thomas Suffern, Jan. 15, 1834, Van Buren Papers.

became a political axiom later, was that the people would return the favor at the polls.[75]

In order to widen the base of his popular support, Van Buren did everything possible to identify himself with Jackson. He believed that Jackson possessed all the attributes of a successful national leader in the eyes of the newly aroused American electorate. He was continually amazed by the fact that, despite the great political risks involved, Jackson's policies were vindicated at the polls. Although not unmindful of his personal popularity, Van Buren believed that Jackson's political strength derived from his forthright and disinterested advocacy of Democratic principles.[76] While personal popularity is difficult to transfer politically, a method of conduct in public office may be repeated, and it was through Jackson that Van Buren sought the pattern and principles upon which to mold himself. He therefore had a stake in protecting Jackson's career and principles from blemish if he was to continue in that tradition himself. "The fate of this administration if not the character of that which is to come after it . . . de-

75. Kendall suggested to Van Buren that Jacksonians woo the Clayites after Jackson's re-election. Van Buren objected on the grounds that the differences between party principles were too great. Kendall replied, saluting Van Buren's "genuine republican principles and inflexibility in maintaining them" but warned the vice-president that a change in Democratic leadership might be necessary. Exchanges such as this one should be kept in mind when one is commenting on Van Buren as a political "trimmer" (Kendall to Van Buren, Nov. 2, 10, 1832, *ibid*).

76. Mahlon Dickerson cautioned Van Buren in January, 1833: "In your St. Tammany Dinner speech, you undertook to prove that our late victory was a triumph of Democratic principles without regard to men. I should be glad to believe it but we must not deceive ourselves. We owed our victory to the personal popularity of General Jackson" (Dickerson to Van Buren, Jan. 11, 1833, Van Buren Papers).

pends upon the result of the great question which now agitates the Country," Van Buren wrote to his son, advising New York Democrats to withdraw their support of any bank plan.[77] Accordingly, Van Buren, more than anyone else, became the "whole hog" Jackson man. As the Jacksonian movement swept on, he became more and more closely identified with it, reaping the advantages of being the committed Jacksonian and supported by the sincere conviction of his own political ideology.

In the Senate in January 1834, Silas Wright presented the resolutions of the New York legislature approving the withdrawal of the deposits. Neither the existing Bank nor any other national bank would be chartered by the administration, Wright claimed; instead the experiment of using state banks as federal depositories would be continued, with emphasis upon monetary reform. Because of Wright's close identification with Van Buren and the administration, his views were taken to be the official party position.[78] Van Buren would have had it no other way. He wrote to his son, "Mr. Wright will present our resolutions tomorrow and will state in doing so the creed by which we mean to stand or fall. I wish Mr. Croswell may follow suit. New York must be in the front ranks in this battle. My hour has come."[79]

The safest conclusion about banking interests during the Jacksonian era is that state bankers were reluctant to inject themselves and their institutions into politics. Other conclusions, though less certain, seem supported by the evidence. In each phase of the administration's Bank War—recharter, re-

77. Van Buren to John Van Buren, Feb. 10, 1834, *ibid.*
78. *Reg. Deb.*, 23 Cong., 1 sess., 397–416; Albany *Argus*, Feb. 5, 1834.
79. Van Buren to John Van Buren, Jan. 29, 1834, Van Buren Papers.

moval, and the post-removal panic—state banks generally did not support the administration. Where there was evidence of state bank support it was on the side of *the* national Bank or *a* national bank. The reason was a very simple one, and readily realized by state bankers: it was merely that the advantages to state banking operations of a national bank outweighed whatever disadvantages might exist in the financial relationship between state and national institutions. Whether as a valuable source of credit and other financial conveniences that only a national bank could provide, or as a regulator of state banking activities, the national Bank was welcomed by state banking interests. The alternative—the absence of a national bank—meant the disintegration of interbank relationships that Biddle had implemented and the withdrawal of an important stabilizing economic force.

The lesson of all this for the Treasury in Washington was clear. The Jacksonians would have to prove to a skeptical banking community that decentralized pet banking operations could offer the same benefits and relatively disinterested regulation previously provided by the national Bank.

3

The Establishment of Pet Banks
and Jacksonian Hard-Money Rhetoric

If the Bank War was not a direct response to the economic ideology of laissez faire with state bank interests leading the way, it might be explained as an extension of the alleged Jacksonian "spoils system" with the larger economic consequences unforeseen. Since it was necessary to use a certain number of banks and to apportion the public money to them on some basis, the possibilities for patronage were extensive. Political benefits to the Jacksonians would result from the economic favor they bestowed upon the selected pets. The political persuasion of a bank's directorate influenced the administration less than a personal recommendation by close friends of the Treasury. It was natural, however, that the reliable bankers whom these friends recommended were mostly Jacksonians; who in turn saw to it that other reliable Jacksonians were among the bank's directors. Not surprisingly, Democratic bankers were well represented among the Treasury pets.[1]

1. Frank Otto Gatell, "Spoils of the Bank War," *American Historical Review*, LXX (1964), 35–58; Harry N. Scheiber, "George Bancroft and the Bank of Michigan, 1837–1841," *Michigan History*, XLIV (1960), 82–90; Scheiber, "A Jacksonian as Banker and Lobbyist: New Light on George Bancroft," *New England Quarterly*, XXXVII (1964), 363–372.

More important than the initial patronage of bank selection was whether Treasury operations would maximize the financial interests of the banks chosen. To what extent would Washington policy respond to the natural cupidity of the pet banks? Pet bankers were not without influence on Treasury management. Secretary Taney was closely allied with important Baltimore banking interests, and Reuben Whitney was related to the Philadelphia pet banker, William D. Lewis, the Girard Bank Cashier. Prior to the Bank veto and deposit removal, both Taney and Whitney recommended actions which showed their involvement with and reliance upon private banking interests.[2]

Much has been written about Taney's role in the Bank War and his personal stake in the outcome because of his connection with Baltimore banking interests.[3] But as Taney's responsibilities increased as Secretary of the Treasury, his view of pet banking operations broadened. Perhaps he had not expected the difficulties he encountered soon after assuming his post. Cornelius W. Lawrence, a Democratic congressman, Bank of America stockholder, and confidant of Taney's, repeatedly and impatiently informed the Bank of America's George Newbold that Taney and those around him in the Treasury underestimated the strength and influence of the BUS on the national economy. He stated further that Taney

2. McFaul and Gatell, "The Outcast Insider: Reuben M. Whitney and the Bank War," *Pennsylvania Magazine of History and Biography*, XCI (1967), 115–144; Bray Hammond, *Banks and Politics*, 335–338; Gatell, "Spoils of the Bank War," 37–38.

3. For Taney's own view see Stuart Bruchey, ed., "Roger Brooke Taney's Account of his Relations with Thomas Ellicott in the Bank War," *Maryland Historical Magazine*, LIII (March, June, 1958), 58–74, 131–152; Carl B. Swisher, *Roger B. Taney* (New York, 1935); Gatell, "Secretary Taney and the Baltimore Pets: A Study in Banking and Politics," *Business History Review*, XXXIX (1965), 205–227.

discounted stories of money market pressure as the lamentations of speculators. "There is a general error here about money matters," Lawrence complained to Newbold.[4]

But Taney was rapidly re-educated in his tenure as Secretary of the Treasury because of the need for developing a viable system invulnerable to political and financial attack. The Secretary increasingly stressed the necessity for financial stability on the part of pet banks and disinterested service by pet bankers. The position of the Bank of America was a case in point. Lawrence was in the habit of transmitting valuable and sometimes privileged information to George Newbold, and undoubtedly helped to solidify the favored position of the Wall Street pet with Secretary Taney. "With the Secretary of the Treasury no Bank stands higher than the Bank of America, and no officer of a Bank higher than yourself," Lawrence joyfully reported to Newbold in December 1833.[5] In return for his Washington services Lawrence expected preferential treatment regarding loans from the Bank of America for his brother's New York firm.[6] But Treasury favoritism toward the Bank of America was more a result of Newbold's conservative management than Lawrence's Washington influence. In January 1834, Lawrence informed Newbold that Taney would allow larger deposits to remain with the Bank of America because the Secretary liked "your *statement*, your *security*, and *whole management* and *conduct*."[7]

The evolution of Treasury favoritism, in the light of political attacks from Congress and the decaying financial influence of the national Bank, was toward those banks and officers

---

4. Lawrence to Newbold, Dec. 21, Nov. 28, 1833, George Newbold Papers, New-York Historical Society.

5. Lawrence to Newbold, Dec. 21, 1833, *ibid.*

6. Lawrence to Newbold, Jan. 27, Feb. 3, 1834, *ibid.*

7. Lawrence to Newbold, Jan. 23, 1834, *ibid.*

promising financial stability rather than political fidelity. Two months after deposit removal, Lawrence told Newbold of Taney's concern over pet bank credit expansion, adding that Taney expected Newbold to take the lead on Wall Street in cautioning the other pet bankers on the matter of loans, especially against lending to speculators and government officers.[8] Taney had already experienced difficulties with his trusted friend and early adviser, Thomas Ellicott of the Union Bank of Maryland, over Ellicott's use of transfer drafts for stock speculation. Under the circumstances it is not surprising that Taney grew to appreciate the financial stability of the conservatively managed Bank of America.

Taney's responsibilities as Secretary of the Treasury also forced him to re-evaluate his Jacksonian prejudices against centralized direction of the economy. Never an advocate of central banking, he nevertheless took halting steps in that direction by urging Congress to pass legislation regulating the public money in the pet banks; to individual pet bankers he stressed restraint in lending policies. To the Planters Bank of Mississippi, Taney wrote that "the first duty of the deposite bank in relation to the public money is to keep itself strong. . . . Too great an extension on the faith of the public deposites is one of the errors most likely to be committed."[9] But moralizing over credit expansion by government officials was no more effective then than it is now and the failure of banks to regulate themselves would lead the administration to recommend congressional regulation.

A distinct advantage of a centralized monetary system is

8. Lawrence to Newbold, Nov. 28, 1833, *ibid.*

9. Taney to Planters Bank of Mississippi, June 2, 1834, Letters to Banks, United States Treasury Papers, National Archives. See also his letters to the Bank of America, Taney to Newbold, Nov. 14, 16, 1833, *Senate Documents,* 23 Cong., 1 sess., no. 16.

that it provides businessmen and others with currency which passes at par throughout the country. This had been one of the most valuable functions of the national Bank system. The Treasury believed that the key to a national currency circulating at par everywhere was specie redemption that was assured and convenient. At the time of removal, Kendall advocated a system of specie concentration in the pet banks of the larger seaboard cities, making all paper currency redeemable there. The specie banks in eastern cities would arrange for credit in European banking houses upon which they could draw when specie was required for export.[10] As Treasury secretary, Taney encouraged more decentralized schemes for monetary stability which depended upon correspondent relationships and mutual redemption among the leading pet banks. The administration press boasted that these voluntary arrangements produced a more stable currency than that formerly provided by the national Bank—a claim vigorously denied by the opposition.[11]

The Treasury's quest for monetary stability led Taney to offer a government guarantee of pet bank notes in receipt for land sales. In the absence of such a guarantee the decision to accept or reject another bank's notes was left to the bank at whose counter the government land receivers presented them. Taney chided the Franklin Bank of Cincinnati on this point, reminding the directors that, as public agents, they should act in the public interest. But the Franklin Bank would not agree unconditionally to accept the notes of other pets until Taney

10. Kendall to William Duane, Sept. 4, 1833, *ibid.,* no. 17.
11. Taney to George Hewes (Commercial Bank of New Orleans), June 24, 1834, Letters to Banks; *Pennsylvanian,* Dec. 6, 1833; Washington *Globe,* Sept. 7, 1835. See the rebuttal by the New York *Journal of Commerce,* Sept. 11, 1835.

extended the government guarantee to cover them.[12] It is significant that one of Levi Woodbury's first acts, upon assuming power as Secretary of the Treasury, was to rescind this government guarantee on the grounds that "its character is somewhat questionable in principle."[13] In a short time, Woodbury, like Taney before him, would be re-educated about the necessity for governmental guidance and influence on the economy.

Imposing reasonable restraints upon state bank credit was only part of the function of a central banking system. An advantage of BUS operations lay in its credit resources, especially beneficial in the western areas of the country. One of Taney's first statements to his pet bankers was designed to convince them that the public moneys they held would replace the credit formerly supplied by the national Bank. One western pet banker, however, wanted assurances from the Treasury that it would stabilize credit resources in his region. If the deposits should be transferred to distant cities, the western pet banker would then have to regulate his discount policy accordingly, and he informed Taney that his bank did not have sufficient capital of its own to finance the large amount of western commodities going to market, especially in view of vanishing BUS credit resources. Taney assured this Cincinnati pet banker that he would take the public interest into

12. The Treasury's guarantee of pet-bank notes was a logical outcome of the Jacksonian belief that the government's unconditional receipt of BUS notes gave them their value (Washington *Globe*, May 17, 1833; Augustus Moore to Taney, April 10, 1834, Letters from Banks; Taney to Moore, April 28, 1834, Letters to Banks; Moore to Taney, May 7, 1834, Letters from Banks). On the same subject see Taney's letters to the Branch Bank of Alabama at Mobile and the Planters Bank of Mississippi, June 21, 1834, Letters to Banks.

13. Woodbury to Franklin Bank of Cincinnati, July 5, 1834, *ibid.*

consideration before ordering any transfers of public money, and stated that while management details were not yet certain, the public deposits would probably provide credit similar to that formerly provided by a branch of the Bank of the United States.[14]

The lessons Taney learned in office evaporated after he returned to Maryland and private life in the summer of 1834. Using his influence with his successor, Levi Woodbury, he was able to prevent any reduction of deposits in the Baltimore pet, the Union Bank;[15] and in November 1835, he wrote to Jackson that he had changed his mind on pet banks regulation. The pet banking experiment "has succeeded to the extent of our most sanguine expectations," he counseled the President, and argued that congressional regulation was unnecessary.[16] In short, a perspective on pet banking operations depended upon the vantage point: the view from the office of the Secretary of the Treasury differed from the one seen from a private home in Maryland.

No individual better fits the stereotype of the self-seeking personal influence peddler than Reuben M. Whitney. Whitney, who supplied the administration with information about BUS affairs, held no official government position but used his experience and contacts with pet bankers, particularly the Girard Bank's William D. Lewis, to play the role of unofficial pet banks coordinator. Because of a personal dislike of Biddle, Whitney encouraged pet bankers to continue the war against the BUS after deposit removal, and advised the Philadelphia Girard Bank to call upon the New York deposit banks for specie in order to force them to cash the Treasury-

14. Augustus Moore to Taney, Nov. 25, 1833, Letters from Banks; Taney to Moore, Dec. 3, 1833, Letters to Banks.

15. Taney to Woodbury, Nov. 5, 6, 1834, Woodbury Papers.

16. Taney to Jackson, Nov. 21, 1835, Jackson Papers.

supplied transfer drafts they held against the Bank of the United States. Taney learned of this action and stopped it immediately, causing Whitney to concede to Lewis, "It might be viewed as vindictive to draw for a million and a half of specie. . . . I have differed with another here, but I do not know but he is right after all. We shall bring them down in time."[17] In another letter to Lewis urging support for the government from the Girard Bank, he wrote, "Pray let nothing prevent the Directors going the *Whole Hog now.* If they will do it, you have not much to fear as to a division of the spoil hereafter."[18]

The "spoil" that Whitney himself expected was a Treasury department appointment as the overseer of pet banking operations, for which there was a real need. The Treasury department was neither staffed nor organized adequately to administer the new financial responsibilities, and Taney was forced to attend to even the most routine correspondence with the deposit banks. The official directly responsible under Taney was the Treasurer of the United States, John Campbell, of the politically influential Campbell family of Virginia and Tennessee. Campbell not only had little overt enthusiasm for the state bank deposit system, but privately had opposed the removal of the deposits and acquiesced only to insure his position.[19] Campbell had allowed the remaining government deposits with the Bank of the United States to dwindle perilously low before informing Taney of the situation, thus forcing the secretary to warn the deposit banks in December 1833 to stand by for government drafts. "The *cause* of calling upon you so early and so suddenly," Whitney informed Lewis, "is

17. Whitney to Lewis, Nov. 13, 14, 15, 1833, Lewis-Neilson Papers.
18. Whitney to Lewis, Nov. 24, 16, 1833, *ibid.*
19. John Campbell to David Campbell, June 5, July 27, 1833, David Campbell Papers, microfilm, Wisconsin Historical Society.

the *necessity* of the case as to the first, and the stupid neglect, *or something else,* of the Treasurer in the second. We are *surrounded by inefficient or unfaithful men.*"[20]

Confident of receiving the appointment as pet banks agent, Whitney drew up a proposal recommending himself, collaborating with William Lewis on the details, and then solicited deposit banks' support. The New York and Boston banks tentatively agreed to the proposal but, significantly, the Union Bank of Maryland held back. Whitney placed the proposal in Taney's hands,[21] but his confidence in the secretary was misplaced. Taney declared that the proposal was unauthorized, and that the department would not act without congressional approval. Even if Congress were to authorize the position, Taney would have opposed Whitney's appointment on the grounds that he did not command the confidence of the financial community. As Taney later summarized this problem to William C. Rives: "I was in the midst of the war —the deposit bankers were for the most part afraid to trust one another and refused to honor each others notes—and thus enabled the opposition and the Bank of the U.S. together to embarrass for a short time the currency—and an agent was of no use to the Department nor of much to the Banks, unless he could command the confidence of all of them."[22] Taney explained to Whitney only that he lacked congressional authorization to appoint a pet banks agent. Left without even "something to pay expenses with," Whitney nevertheless ex-

20. Whitney to Lewis, Dec. 17, 1833, Lewis-Neilson Papers.
21. *House Committee Reports,* 24 Cong., 2 sess., no. 193, 17–18, 255–256, 185–186; Whitney to Jackson, Oct. 6, 1834, Jackson Papers.
22. *House Committee Reports,* 24 Cong., 2 sess., no. 193, 140–141; Taney to Rives, April 16, 1836, William C. Rives Papers, Library of Congress.

pected to receive the Treasury post eventually. "I suppose if I was to *insist*, I could have what I want *now*," he lamented to Lewis. "I should feel perfectly satisfied, but that I want money in my purse."[23]

Taney's reluctance to appoint an agent without congressional approval vanished as pet bank operations required more and more supervision, but he passed over Whitney for the job, proposing instead George Newbold. If Newbold were to refuse, Taney preferred one of the Girard Bank officials. But Whitney's confidence was still unshaken: "Now let who will come, I shall have to do the whole of the business, *sub rosa*, and so it is understood," he wrote to Lewis.[24] No deposit bank official could afford to leave his bank during the financial difficulties of the 1833–1834 winter, however, and no agent was appointed during Taney's term as Secretary of the Treasury.[25]

When the Senate refused its consent to Taney's appointment and Jackson appointed Levi Woodbury to the post in the summer of 1834, Whitney saw his opportunity and renewed his proposal to Woodbury. The new secretary, however, agreed with his predecessor's interpretation of the department's lack of authority to appoint an agent and suggested to Whitney that the deposit banks initiate the appointment. In his letter Woodbury assured Whitney that the department would cooperate with any agent selected by the deposit banks.[26] Whether Woodbury intended it as a recommendation to the banks or not, Whitney realized the value of the correspondence and used it as such in applying to them.

23. Whitney to Lewis, Nov. 12, 1833, Lewis-Neilson Papers.
24. Whitney to Lewis, Dec. 17, 1833, *ibid*.
25. Taney to Rives, April 16, 1836, Rives Papers.
26. Woodbury to Whitney, Nov. 5, 1834, in *House Committee Reports*, 24 Cong., 2 sess., no. 193, 437–438.

Through Lewis, Whitney was appointed as the agent for the Girard Bank.[27] But the effectiveness of a pet banks agent depended upon his being hired by the other large-capital eastern banks, whose cooperation he could not rely upon as readily as that of the faithful Girard. Therefore, as leverage with the Boston and New York pets, an unsigned letter was sent to David Henshaw in Boston with a copy to New York. The letter was allegedly written "by a person . . . high in the confidence of the Executive." It urged the banks to hire a Washington coordinator; to aid in their decision the letter closed with this thought: "The President and Secretary of the Treasury, I know, view the subject in the same light that I do, and will be gratified if the banks will establish such an agency; and, from his talents, experience, and fidelity, no appointment would be more acceptable to them than that of Mr. Whitney, who has already been recommended to the department."[28] Kendall actually wrote the anonymous letter, but Whitney later advised Lewis: "To you, I can say, that it has not been written without consulting those to whom it refers."[29]

Whitney was finally employed regularly by twenty of the deposit banks, and others paid him on an irregular basis for the financial reports he formulated on the condition of all the deposit banks. Many of the banks undoubtedly employed him in the belief, as implied in Kendall's letter, that it was the wish of Jackson and Woodbury that they do so and probably hoped in return to receive a larger share of the deposits. As their agent Whitney attempted to keep the number of deposit banks small so that those employing him would not have to share the government funds with others. He also worked to

27. Whitney to Lewis, Nov. 6, 1834, Lewis to Whitney, Nov. 10, 1834, in *ibid.*, 448–450.

28. *Ibid.*, 534–535.

29. Whitney to Lewis, Nov. 6, 8, 1834, Lewis-Neilson Papers.

ward off severe congressional restrictions on the banks. That he failed in both attempts indicates the limited extent of his alleged influence.

If Whitney's career served only to illustrate the Jacksonian "spoils system" at work, it might make an interesting footnote to the history of the era, but his actions as pet banks agent reveal much about the system itself. There is no need to theorize about Whitney's ambitions and intentions: his conversion to Jacksonianism was designed to benefit him personally. The pet banks system offered grand opportunities for himself and for the pet bankers whose wishes he hoped to translate into Treasury policy. But it very quickly developed that the responsibilities for managing the public money, coupled with the emerging anti-banking tendencies on the part of Jacksonians, would thwart Whitney's efforts. While never embracing the hard-money policy of the Jacksonians, he realized that his position depended upon preserving the usefulness and stability of state banking operations.[30] Whitney knew his "place" and, as will be shown, employed Jacksonian rhetoric in scolding bankers about their duty to reform the currency and restrain their credit activities.

In the chaotic aftermath of deposit removal, most Democrats supported the administration's pet banks system as a necessary alternative to a national bank, while the newly-formed Whig party called it a vast patronage empire of Jacksonian banks that would lead the nation to economic disaster. Democrats, in an attempt to deny that the administration desired exclusive control of the public funds, challenged Whigs to enact congressional regulation of pet banking. Important to the immediate stability of the pet banking system was the reversal of Biddle's credit contraction, brought about through

30. McFaul and Gatell, "The Outcast Insider," *Pennsylvania Magazine of History and Biography*, XCI (1967), 115–144.

pressure from the business community. Crucial political support was demonstrated by the passage of House resolutions in April 1834, which endorsed deposit removal and sanctioned the use of state banks as public depositories.[31] With credit relaxed and hopes of reversing Jacksonian policy diminishing, the pet banking experiment began to look more and more like a permanent part of the Jackson administration.

The Democrats moved to take full advantage of their accomplishments. Aside from the rhetoric celebrating the heroic struggle against the "Monster," Jacksonians were aware that the return of prosperity would pay political dividends and be attributed to the pet bank experiment. One of Congressman James K. Polk's constituents listed the ingredients for future Jacksonian political victories: "A full crop, plentiful money market and success of the State Banks will prepare the way for a cordial support on the part of the people."[32] Indeed, Secretary Taney's report to Congress on the country's financial state in June 1834 was so optimistic that the Whigs attempted to stop its reading in the Senate.[33] Pointing to the country's prosperity and the role of state banks in maintaining that prosperity became a Democratic ritual, proof that a national bank was unnecessary. In House debate Polk saluted the national prosperity and pointed out to his colleagues that the Bank had not died in vain: "The Country, then, has been prosperous but she is indebted for that prosperity neither to the bank nor to the panic, but to the new impulses springing

31. Govan, *Nicholas Biddle*, 251–259. The House resolutions in April 1834 against the Bank and approving the governmental use of state banks ended the uncertainty over possible changes in Treasury policy (*House Journal*, 23 Cong., 1 sess., 483–486; Washington *Globe*, April 10, 1834).

32. S. Smith to Polk, Sept. 11, 1834, James K. Polk Papers, Library of Congress.

33. *Register of Debates*, 23 Cong., 1 sess., 2007–2008.

out of the employment of State banks as fiscal agents of the Government."[34]

Under the popular leadership of General Jackson, Democrats could celebrate the death of the "Monster," point to the growing economy with pride, and indignantly deny opposition charges about spoils of office and personal influence in pet banking. Taney, resting comfortably in Baltimore, was sure that the "sufficiency" of pet banking had been proven. Reuben Whitney spoke jubilantly of the Democratic victory in New York in the fall of 1834: "It shows that the *People* have come forward to the rescue and to sustain the last great measure of General Jackson's Administration, the removal of the deposits."[35] The great crusade was over and Jacksonians were confident that they were entitled to the political rewards of a grateful public and a well-earned rest from political battles.

But there were irresistible movements within American political and economic life which upset this formula for stability. One resulted from the necessity for Democrats to distinguish themselves politically from Whigs in the aftermath of the Bank War. As a result of the assault on the BUS, the anti-banking character of Jacksonian Democracy was of crucial importance in this process of political definition. Reuben Whitney, at the same time that he was celebrating deposit removal as "the last great measure" of the administration, warned Lewis that "those of us who have been opposing the BUS, have now got to take care that the impetus of opposition to that institution does not extend too far, and injure the State bank interest."[36] Such political hostility toward banks reinforced those Democrats demanding more restrictive regu-

34. *Ibid.*, 23 Cong., 2 sess., 1440.
35. Whitney to Lewis, Nov. 8, 1834, Lewis-Neilson Papers.
36. Whitney to Lewis, Nov. 6, 1834, *ibid.*

lations; together these two forces exerted a significant influence upon Treasury management of pet banks. At the same time, the Treasury had to consider the inflationary demands of its many critics.

The advocacy of hard money was put forth by Democrats, either with true conviction or in order to satisfy the different and sometimes conflicting forces within the Jacksonian movement. Nominal support for hard money was a small enough price for business-minded Jacksonians to pay for the larger rewards of pet banking. Other Jacksonians could ease their guilt over these same rewards by honestly and vigorously supporting currency reform. In the abstract, as Marvin Meyers has shown, hard money evoked images of stabilization, welcomed in a period of rapid change.[37] Moreover, the term was employed as a political symbol to define the differences between Whigs and Democrats.

The partnership between the Democratic administration and state banks required by pet banking policy placed the Jacksonians in the unenviable political position of giving aid and comfort to the banking interest. But if the Jacksonian goal was hard money, then the use of state banks would be excusable as a necessary tactical means to the reformist end. Frank Blair's *Globe* made exactly this point when it editorialized somewhat defensively in the summer of 1834 that Jackson's "hostility to the Bank of the United States proceeded from no design on his part to create a spurious paper currency on state credit."[38] Instead the *Globe* had decreed the month before that "the name of Jackson is now identified with metallic currency."[39] The administration's critics attacked its hard-money policy on two fronts. Advocating hard money, they claimed, was a hastily contrived political device to cover the

37. Marvin Meyers, *Jacksonian Persuasion*, ch. 2.
38. Washington *Globe*, Aug. 26, 1834.   39. *Ibid.*, July 15, 1834.

financial failures of pet banking operations. At the same time they warned the public of the seriousness of the Jacksonian commitment to hard money, portraying Democrats as visionaries attempting to throw themselves against the irresistible force of a credit-fed and steam-driven economy. In short, the Jacksonians were attacked by their critics as being both political opportunists and irresponsible idealists.[40]

Both tendencies were present, as they often are in American politics. Many Jacksonians were sincere about hard money while others used it as an excuse for their favoritism toward state banks. Nevertheless, pet banks found themselves promoted to the front lines in the Jacksonian crusade for economic reform. Jackson stated at the time of removal that by receiving federal funds the state banks "will oblige themselves to come into certain arrangements." A few months later he argued that the use of state banks would allow the administration to "introduce a metallic currency throughout the Union." The *Globe* echoed these sentiments, emphasizing that the public deposits would be used "to encourage the gradual suppression of the issues of small bank notes." Churchill C. Cambreleng, New York City Democratic congressman, defended the administration's use of state banks against anti-banking extremists urging a separation of the government from all banking, by claiming that the administration could make the pets "instrumental in the great work which has been so successfully commenced, of reform in our currency."[41]

Originally portrayed only as feasible financial alternatives to a national bank, state banks were now called upon to re-

40. See the speeches of Webster and Clay in *Register of Debates*, 23 Cong., 1 sess., 644, 1433.
41. Jackson to James Hamilton, Sept. 8, 1833, Feb. 2, 1834, in Hamilton, *Reminiscences*, 269–270; Washington *Globe*, March 28, 1834; *Register of Debates*, 23 Cong., 2 sess., 1305–1306.

form the currency. It is this metamorphosis which explains the Jacksonian condemnation of state banking after the general banking suspension in the spring of 1837. Whether the Jacksonian anti-bank outburst in 1837 is taken as an irrational belief in a banking conspiracy or as the need for a convenient scapegoat for their financial folly, the reasons are traceable to the Jacksonian rhetoric which defined governmental use of state banks as the easiest, most convenient method of currency reform. Woe unto the banks if they betrayed this noble purpose.

Another function of the Jacksonian hard-money rhetoric was to promise economic and consequently social stability. Lack of stability was, of course, a reflection of the real problem which lay in the economic dynamics of the capitalist system. Jacksonians did not seriously challenge that system, either because they did not understand its operation, or because of their economic conservatism, but they did hope to stabilize the economy by preventing "its ruinous fluctuations arising from alternate expansions and contractions of bank issues," as Virginia Senator William C. Rives expressed it.[42] Taney, in a Maryland speech, claimed that with the suppression of small notes, "we shall have no reason to apprehend the fluctuations and disasters to which the sudden expansions and contractions of our paper currency has [sic] heretofore been liable."[43]

Economic fluctuation hurt the laboring man in particular, Jacksonians argued, and he would benefit the most from currency reform. The *Globe* argued that, with hard money in circulation, the laboring man "would be effectually protected against all the casualties and frauds of paper money." On the other hand, financiers and moneyed men need not stay awake

42. *Register of Debates,* 23 Cong., 1 sess., 264–265.
43. Washington *Globe,* Oct. 1, 1834.

nights worrying about the Jacksonian revolution. "For large transactions and commercial purposes Banks and Bank paper should be permitted to exist," Blair assured the administration's critics. "The evils of banking would be thus curtailed, and its risks thrown upon that part of society which profits by it, and is most able to bear occasional losses."[44] The Jacksonian conception of monetary reform promised benefits to both rich and poor.

The issue of hard money gave Democrats a sense of political direction and a distinctive rhetoric after the Bank War. Party images, created to a great extent by the confrontation between Jackson and the "Monster," lost their sharpness as Whigs hurried to separate themselves from the BUS cause. Whig Senator Thomas Ewing was advised during the "panic session" that reliance on the Bank was backfiring. It was "a heavy weight to carry and keep with it popular sentiment," he was warned. The Democrats had done their job so well on the "Monster" that the Whigs were ready to abandon, at least in political campaigns, their advocacy of the discredited institution. "Several of the old U.S. Bank friends gave her up today for *dead*," one Democratic congressman wrote to Gideon Welles as Congress adjourned in the summer of 1834. The relationship of the Whig party to the Bank came under close scrutiny at the end of the year as Whigs sustained further defeats at the polls. "After staggering along from year to year, with a doomed Bank upon our shoulders, both the Bank and our party are finally overwhelmed," was the post-election comment of Thurlow Weed's *Albany Evening Journal*. "The burthen, however, is now removed," the *Journal* concluded. A prominent Philadelphia Whig lawyer agreed with this assessment of the relationship between the BUS cause and Whig

44. *Ibid.*, March 29, 1834.

political fortunes. "The sooner we get rid of it the better," was his advice to Senator Willie P. Mangum.[45]

During 1835 the Whigs gradually abandoned the Bank's cause on the democratic grounds that the people had spoken against it at the polls. Biddle wrote to Webster in surprise and regret when the Bank's most powerful advocate joined this chorus of Whig dissenters. "Now I doubt very much whether public opinion can be said to have declared against the Bank —but supposing it to be so, what jarred upon the minds of the friends of the Bank . . . was that you should have pronounced such a sentence. It seemed to imply an indifference— a coldness—an alienation from the Bank and a desire to disconnect yourself with it."[46] Biddle understood as well as any other voter the effect Webster hoped to achieve.

Some Democrats worried over the lack of differences between a Democrat and a Whig dissociated from the Bank. John Niles advised a fellow Connecticut Democrat that New York Whigs were looking for an anti-Bank candidate for governor, and Van Buren warned another New Yorker that the Whigs' "next cognomen will be Democrats—remember what I say."[47] Some Democrats resisted Whig strategy and even while arranging the burial of the "Monster" planned a resurrection every election year. Isaac Hill, New Hampshire Democratic Senator, argued that "the question of Bank or no

45. C. Hammond to Ewing, March 27, 1834, Ewing Papers, Library of Congress; H. Ellsworth to Welles, June 24, 1834, Welles Papers, Library of Congress; *Albany Evening Journal*, Nov. 15, 1834; J. Randall to Mangum, Dec. 12, 1834, in Henry T. Shanks, ed., *The Papers of Willie Person Mangum* (4 vols.; Raleigh, N.C., 1950–1955), II, 236.

46. Biddle to Webster, April 6, 1835, Biddle Papers.

47. J. Niles to Welles, Aug. 3, 1834, Welles Papers; Van Buren to Jesse Hoyt, Oct. 21, 1834, in William L. Mackenzie, *Life and Times of Martin Van Buren* (Boston, 1846), 257.

Bank, as dividing the two great political parties, will be precisely the question that Democrats should most desire." Van Buren advised Jackson: "The opposition labor hard to shake off the Bank, but we are determined to hold them to it"; and Benton, in a reply to an invitation honoring Taney declared, "Every election State or Federal, now and for years to come, will be contested upon the question of *Bank or no Bank*."[48]

But the battles of the Bank War already had a musty air about them, like heroic tales old soldiers tell at their clubs. The threat of BUS recharter was losing its potency and Democratic rhetoric associating Whigs with the institution becoming less and less meaningful. The opportunity for a new symbol of party division was at hand, however, in the hard-money cause. The *Globe* announced that hard money would be the test of parties. "*Gold* and *paper* will become badges of parties, like the red and white roses were formerly in England. A man will soon be known as belonging to the *Gold party*, or the *Paper party*." It is not Blair's enthusiasm that is interesting, but rather his awareness of the political opportunities of hard-money rhetoric. "Here then is a new war to entertain the public in the recess of Congress—the war of *paper* against *gold!* the war of the *bank* of the US against the *mint* of the US!" New heroes and new "monsters" were in the process of being formed.[49]

But political parties, like people, are often influenced by their own self-descriptions. Democratic rhetoric praising hard money, regardless of the motives behind it, influenced political reality. The administration sponsored legislation imposing restraints upon bank notes of small denomination. When the

48. I. Hill to Welles, April 11, 1834, Welles Papers; Van Buren to Jackson, July 2, 1834, in *Correspondence of Andrew Jackson*, V, 274; Washington *Globe*, Aug. 27, 1834.

49. Washington *Globe*, July 15, 1834.

legislation failed in Congress, the Treasury initiated action on its own authority. In March 1835, Secretary Woodbury ordered all pet banks to refuse in receipt for government dues any bank note under $5 in denomination after September 1835, a similar ban covering all notes under $10 to take effect after March 1836.[50] This Treasury circular imposed milder restraint on banking operations than the administration's defeated bill would have required. James Polk, in sponsoring the bill in Congress, had explained that the government intended to have pet banks refuse the notes of any denomination from a bank that continued to issue bank notes under $5 and then $10 in denomination.[51]

A combination of circumstances produced the Treasury circular. The economic pressure had eased by the summer of 1834 and support for deflationary measures was increasing. Jackson-Benton hard-money Democrats were becoming impatient to make gold and silver currency a reality, especially since congressional bank regulation had been defeated twice in Congress. Finally, self-interested advocates of pet banking realized that Treasury use of state banks depended upon their cooperating with the administration in currency reform. In fact, Reuben Whitney had as much to do with the issuance of the circular as anyone. In a detailed letter to Woodbury, he urged departmental action restricting bank notes of small denomination. His letter contained specific suggestions about when the small-note ban should go into effect and for what amounts, suggestions which Woodbury followed closely in his formal circular. The conclusion of Whitney's letter revealed his reasoning: "The reform of the currency appears to be a measure connected with and following the removal of the deposites, and the employment of the State Banks as the

50. *Senate Documents*, 24 Cong., 1 sess., no. 2.
51. *Register of Debates*, 23 Cong., 2 sess., 1274.

fiscal agents of the government." Whitney was slow to realize this connection, but alert enough to see that his interests and the interests of the pet banks lay in cooperating with Treasury reforms.[52] Whitney explained this strategy in his own circular to the deposit banks. He encouraged pet bankers to "express a willingness to enter into such an arrangement." The reform was a needed check on the economy, he explained, but more important, would "lead to causing all the banks which unite in carrying out this measure to obtain increased and extended popularity." In return for their cooperation, Whitney suggested that bankers request protection from hostile congressional legislation.[53] Clearly, Whitney's plan was to urge the deposit banks to assume the role of indispensable agents in reforming the currency while still retaining the advantages of the government deposits.

But did the advantages of the government deposits to the banks outweigh the disadvantages of currency reform? Thomas Ellicott in February 1834 had urged caution on Taney regarding Democratic advocacy of currency reform. "Let us not attempt to move too fast but wait for further developments—it will all come out right," he advised.[54] The bankers' replies to Woodbury's Treasury circular were equally cautious. Their responses may be summarized as follows. Banning notes under $5 would be no great handicap since many states already prohibited their circulation. Banning notes under $10 would require what one banker termed "a careful examination." It would have little effect and be discriminatory unless all state banks were denied the privilege of issuing notes under $10. Many of the banks frankly stated that the advantages of the government deposits were not great

52. Whitney to Woodbury, March 22, 1835, Woodbury Papers.
53. *House Committee Reports*, 24 Cong., 2 sess., nos. 193, 413–415.
54. Ellicott to Taney, Feb. 20, 1834, Perine Papers.

enough to warrant such a sacrifice. As the president of the Union Bank of Tennessee put it, "To induce the state banks generally to come into the arrangement I presume it will have to be made their interest to do so," and another banker replied that he would be unwilling to ban notes under $10 unless "advantages are to result from the measure, which have not been perceived or anticipated by us." The banks also followed Whitney's suggestion in replying that in return for their cooperation they expected to be protected from restrictive congressional legislation.[55] Though the pet bankers were grumbling, and hard-money advocates were not satisfied either, at least the administration had made clear that it expected state banks used as federal depositories to be something more than simply an alternative to a national bank.

The administration's actions during the early months of the pet banking "experiment" demonstrate that more was involved in the Bank War than an extension of the spoils system to state banks and an eagerness to satisfy the entrepreneurial impulses allegedly concentrated in these institutions. Jacksonian purposes and intentions after the Bank War may seem unclear because Democrats were moving confusedly toward monetary stability through restrictions on state banking. The administration's relative ineffectiveness in achieving these goals, demonstrated by the state bankers' lukewarm response to the Treasury circular, increased Democratic demands for more vigorous action. A plan to harness anti-bank hostility to Democratic demands for bank regulation was the Jacksonians' best hope for success in currency reform, but such an alliance posed a political problem. The exercise of governmental power, so demonstrably required to regulate the economy

55. See the numerous pet bank replies to Woodbury's Treasury circular in the Treasury files for April and May, 1835, Letters from Banks.

properly, was incompatible with the Jacksonian ideology of laissez faire. A temporary expedient, described in the next chapter, lay in their advocacy of state legislation; ultimately, however, Democrats would be forced to develop a national policy which clearly and forcefully defined national responsibilities for banking and the economy. As subsequent chapters will show, Democratic efforts to meet these responsibilities brought into the open the divergent tendencies within the Jacksonian coalition, moved most Democrats to a stronger anti-bank posture, and contributed to Van Buren's defeat in 1840.

4

Democrats and State Regulation

A way of partially reconciling Jacksonian political theory
with the demands of economic reality rose out of the nature
of the federal system itself. With banking under state jurisdiction, economic regulation could be relegated to the state
level while federal responsibilities were confined to moral
suasion and exemplary conduct.[1] It is surely one of the great
luxuries of the federal system that power can be sanctimon-
iously denied at the same time that it is being energetically
pursued.

Frank Blair's editorials from the fall of 1833 through 1834
urged Democrats to capture state governments and regulate
state banking. Despite the *Globe's* motto, "The World is

1. Kendall assured John Niles of Connecticut that "a principal
part of the real reforms which our government requires, must be
carried into effect by the state governments" (Kendall to Niles,
May 13, 1835, Welles Papers). The Washington *Globe* urged Jacksonians in Congress to impose exemplary restrictions on District of
Columbia banks as a guide for state action (Washington *Globe*, May
30, 1836). Jackson proposed that Congress charter a new bank in the
District "upon real banking principles, such as will be a model for
the States" (Jackson to Kendall, Nov. 24, 1836, in *Correspondence of
Andrew Jackson*, V, 438–439). Jackson's suggestion was publicized
by the *Globe* the next month (Washington *Globe*, Dec. 31, 1836).
Jacksonian moralizing about correct banking principles for the District of Columbia was based on the naive assumption that state banking reform only awaited national guidance and example.

Governed too Much," Blair and other Democrats were not so doctrinaire as to adhere slavishly to any theory when they felt it hindered necessary action. "We are not among those who are for increasing the powers of any Government," Blair began an editorial in November 1833, but he went on to advocate increasing "the prerogatives of the Government to the very limits of the Constitution . . . when an attempt is made by an arrogant monied aristocracy to set itself above the constituted authorities of the people at large."[2] He argued that state banking abuses arose because the people and state legislature had left things alone, charging that the opposition, despite their advocacy of a national bank, "contrive to get control of every State institution which is composed exclusively of private stockholders." The remedy, as he saw it, was to have the public exercise some control over state banking. "If the people, are ever to enjoy benefit from the *banking privilege* conferred on corporations, the State must always participate in the emolument, as the principle stockholder, and in its management by having (with the President) a majority in the board of directors."[3] Blair distinguished between state banks

2. Washington *Globe*, Nov. 16, 1833.

3. *Ibid.*, May 28, 1833. Of course, state-owned banks could expand bank credit as easily as privately owned banks; naturally they were not advocated on hard-money grounds. The state-owned bank in Georgia and the proposal for a state-owned bank in Maryland were supported because the states needed additional banking capital, and Blair's praise for the newly chartered State Bank of Indiana in December 1834 was in the spirit of state support of credit, rather than restriction. He lauded the "parental care with which the Government provides for the wants of its young and growing population out of the resources flowing from the riches and credit of the State, which has drawn together the capital of the Bank" (Milton S. Heath, *Constructive Liberalism: The Role of the State in Economic Development in Georgia to 1860* [Cambridge, 1954], 190–195; Bryan, "State Banking in Maryland," 82–85; Washington *Globe*, Dec. 19, 1834).

partially owned and/or controlled by the state and private state banks chartered with relatively unrestricted privileges, saving his praise for the former.

Advocates of Jacksonian banking policy, although their motives were not always clear, increasingly sought greater public responsibility for banking as opposed to a system of "special privileges." This is not to say that Democrats did not hunger for private bank charters as much as Whigs, or that Democrats were not associated with private banks—clearly they were. But Democratic rhetoric moved toward increased public control over banking; where actions did not follow, there was enough of a conflict to cause deep rifts within the party regarding banking policy.

Public control or regulation of banking was as ambiguous a concept as that of hard money, especially at a time when the changing character of commercial banking made it difficult to know what practices needed controlling. Democratic policy pointed the way to the most simplistic form of state action— the elimination of small-denomination bank notes. A sterner test of state allegiance to the Jacksonian cause lay in the curtailment of bank expansion. Neither of these solutions was satisfactory, however, economically or politically. Eliminating small-denomination bank notes represented a kind of hard-money tokenism, relatively insignificant in itself and only partially successful in achieving responsible banking regulation. Furthermore, prohibiting banks in one state from issuing low-denomination bank notes created a vacuum rapidly filled by notes of banks in other states. Such a reform, whatever its economic benefits, was only realistic if undertaken voluntarily by all states (an unlikely possibility) or imposed through federal legislation—a course which raised serious political problems.

Jacksonian banking policy faced even greater difficulties

over the question of state bank expansion. In states where Jacksonians were in firm control of the legislative machinery, they were tempted by the logic of their own rhetoric to refuse additional bank charters. This proved to be a difficult position to maintain for two reasons. First, as population and commercial opportunities expanded, it was unrealistic to refuse to increase banking facilities. If common sense was not persuasive on this point, the competitive challenge from other states which were increasing their own banking facilities would convince the legislature that banking expansion was necessary for commercial success. Second, there was the political danger that legislative refusal to charter additional banks would be interpreted as favoritism toward the existing banks. Whether true or not (and there was always enough evidence to make such an allegation appear credible), such charges were powerful political weapons.

In terms of rhetoric and moral righteousness, Jacksonians functioned best out of office, when all the sins of politics and banking could be attributed to the opposition. The problem with this approach was that it often convinced the electorate: then the "bank party" was thrown out and the Democrats rose to power. Apostasy was almost immediate among some former Democratic bank foes who became overt bank friends provoking sermons about the frailties of human nature and the corruptions of public office. Sentiment among conscience-stricken Democrats then increased for abandoning banking to its own excesses and cutting once and for all the cord of corruption between political action and private gain. Naturally bankers were willing enough to cooperate in withdrawing banking from the political arena and to assume greater responsibility for their own affairs.

Obviously there were exceptions. In some states political control and responsibility for banking increased rather than

decreased after the Panic of 1837,[4] and Washington Jacksonians attempted to make federal regulation a part of their independent treasury bill.[5] Nevertheless Democratic rhetoric
in the post-Panic period relied more and more on explaining
the natural and mutually beneficial advantages to be gained
from divorcing political power from banking activities. A
few examples of the interaction of Democratic politics and
state banking will illustrate this development and reveal problems on the state level similar to those confronted by Washington Jacksonians trying to cope with the reality of banking
under changing Jacksonian rhetoric.[6]

A recent study by Donald Cole shows that New Hampshire
politics during the Jacksonian era were characterized by partisan and often bitter debate over issues. Cole finds that there
was continuity in New Hampshire politics between the first
and second party systems, with former Federalists voting for
the National Republicans in 1828. The voting turnout being
unusually high for New England, Cole concludes that the
Bank War was a real issue to the voters in New Hampshire,
and that those voters were divided along socioeconomic lines
with poor farm areas supporting the Democrats and the more
prosperous areas voting Whig. In New Hampshire, at least,
the Jacksonians were sincere reformers, representing the

4. James Roger Sharp, *The Jacksonians versus the Banks: Politics
in The States After the Panic of 1837* (New York, 1970).

5. See Ch. 7 for an analysis of the independent treasury proposal.

6. A recent study of legislative behavior on banking and currency
issues in selected states supports the views presented here. While
Democrats were divided over these issues, Whigs consistently supported bank and other forms of corporate expansion. Democrats
achieved a firmer anti-bank unity after the Panic of 1837 and were
always united on the issue of restricting small denomination bank
notes (Herbert Ershkowitz and William G. Shade, "Consensus or
Conflict? Political Behavior in the State Legislatures during the
Jacksonian Era," *Journal of American History* (Dec. 1971) 591–621.

lower classes, and issues were important. Contrary to entre-preneurial conclusions, Cole finds that New Hampshire Democrats, although not anti-capitalist radicals, took political action in the 1840's which arrested the state's economic growth. Democrats took the lead in restricting banking practices by imposing specie reserves, establishing bank commissioners, and even attempting to curtail the limited liability clause in bank charters.[7]

Connecticut is another example of a New England state where the banking issue, if not paramount, nevertheless played a significant role in state politics. The Connecticut Democracy was divided between two factions: one was led by Gideon Welles and John Niles and the other gathered around the Democratic bank and government pet, the Farmers and Mechanics Bank in New Haven, presided over by James Dodd. The Welles-Niles faction was on the whole sympathetic to the Washington anti-bank posture of national Democrats, while the Dodd faction was just as vigorously nonideological in its political attitudes.[8]

Some of the controversy between the two groups centered on patronage rewards from Washington. In 1835 John Niles had moved to the United States Senate from his important federal appointment as Postmaster. Welles, who had expected to receive the vacated position, was challenged by the supporters of James Dodd. Welles was prepared to use his position as editor of the Hartford *Times* to expose the Dodd clique's infidelity to true Jacksonianism, but Washington

7. Donald B. Cole, *Jacksonian Democracy in New Hampshire, 1800–1851* (Cambridge, 1970), 72–81, chs. 5 and 6, on the Bank War and the 1832 election, and 192–193, 214–215.

8. The Gideon Welles Papers are a rich source for an analysis of the Connecticut Democracy. On the factional banking dispute see B. L. Raynor to Welles, Aug. 1, 1833; Welles to Isaac Hill, undated; M. Gardner to Welles, June 24, 1834, Welles Papers.

counseled peace. Isaac Hill, the U.S. Senator from New Hampshire, reassured Welles regarding the Postmaster appointment and cautioned that intraparty squabbles could only weaken the Democratic cause. After urging political expediency on Welles, Hill felt called upon to reaffirm his own fidelity to true Jacksonianism: "I will not go a single step to increase banks, to renew charters, or to extend bank privileges." Silas Wright also urged restraint on Welles, arguing that any attack on a pet bank would strengthen the Whig demands for an end to the pet banks system.[9]

Though Connecticut Democrats improved their state legislative standing in the 1836 elections and the political position of Welles and his allies was apparently strengthened, it still remained to be seen whether the Welles brand of anti-bank Jacksonianism could be translated into state action. The previous Connecticut legislature, despite a Democratic majority, had imposed a ban only on bank notes at $3 denomination and below, rather than the usual $5 or $10 prohibition. After spearheading an investigation into state banking, Connecticut Democrats narrowly passed a bill for the repeal of one of the state banks, only to see the effort thwarted by the veto of a Democratic governor. State bank supporters within the party were a "curse to democracy," one of Welles' correspondents lamented, "but how shall we get rid of them is the question?"[10]

9. Hill to Welles, Nov. 29, 1834; Hill to Niles, Feb. 21, 1835; S. Kellog to Niles, Dec. 15, 1835; Niles to Welles, Feb. 5, 1836; Hill to Welles, Jan. 12, 1836; Wright to Welles, Jan. 8, 1836, Welles Papers.

10. For the 1836 election results see *Niles Register*, April 16, 1836. On the plans to extend the small-note ban and other bank reforms, see Niles to Welles, April 8, 1836, Welles Papers; William F. Hasse, Jr., *A History of Banking in New Haven Connecticut* (New Haven, 1946), 24–25; Jarvis M. Morse, *A Neglected Period of Connecticut's History, 1818–1850* (New Haven, 1939), 303; C. Douglas to Welles, Feb. 11, 1836, Welles Papers.

Disappointed Democrats called for fresh mandates from an allegedly anti-bank electorate. At the end of the 1836 state legislative session, one of Welles' correspondents wrote, "I do hope that the People will see to it next spring, to send agents to the Assembly who are not only opposed to making more banks, but in favor of keeping a tight rein upon those already in existence." More and more, however, the remedy for Democratic hypocrisy and disunity over banking seemed to lie not in electing more principled anti-bank Democrats to office but rather in dissolving the connection between banks and politics. Even Welles' correspondent who urged a "tight rein" upon banking saw no contradiction between this position and his hope that "the day of chartered monopolies will soon pass by and one of free trade and people's rights speedily dawn upon the land."[11]

The disunity within the Democratic party in Connecticut was not unusual in itself; political parties on the state level are rarely free of bickering and highly publicized struggles for power. The significance of the Connecticut conflict lies in how the banking issue polarized the dispute, for the true test of Jacksonianism was one's attitude toward banks. Some Democrats resisted, arguing that Washington banking policy should have nothing to do with Connecticut politics. Nevertheless, the Welles-Niles group insisted upon defining party fidelity in these terms and was supported by Washington Jacksonians (except at election times) in this effort. But the failure of the Connecticut Democracy to deal effectively either

---

11. G. Mansfield to Welles, Dec. 31, 1836. Welles had already corresponded with Churchill Cambreleng, the New York City Democrat, about Connecticut's banking system, and the latter, after suggesting various reforms, added: "You know my opinion to be that government ought to have nothing to do with banking" (C. Cambreleng to Welles, April 15, 1835, Welles Papers).

with bank supporters within the party or bank operations within the state inevitably led the party's most articulate spokesmen to advocate a separation of banking and government. In this sense there is a very real connection between Connecticut and Washington Jacksonians: they each struggled against the "banking interest" and each, in the long run, favored a divorce between banking and politics.

In the state of Maryland no rigid ideological-economic pattern can be discerned in the political conflicts between Jacksonians and their opponents. The most recent study of the early Jacksonian party in the state concludes that it was made up primarily of ambitious, opportunistic politicians who clung frantically to Jackson's coattails. Maryland politicians might continue to laud the personal virtues of the Old Hero, but as his administration was identified more and more with certain economic positions, Washington policy began to have an effect on Maryland politics.[12]

The economic disruptions which followed the Bank War led to a Whiggish coalition assuming state power in Maryland in 1834. This Whig-dominated legislature increased the state's banking capital by approximately $17 million and approved the creation of nine new Baltimore banks. Democratic opposition, even if serious, would have been futile. Actually, the state needed additional banking capital and the newly chartered banks were conservatively and responsibly managed. It was not banking per se that divided Maryland Democrats from Whigs; it was the discipline to be imposed upon state banking practices. When the Whigs offered a legislative ban on bank notes under $5 denomination, Democrats countered with an amendment to raise the prohibition to all notes below $10 denomination. After this amendment was defeated Demo-

12. Mark H. Haller, "The Rise of the Jackson Party in Maryland, 1820–1829," *Journal of Southern History*, XXVIII (1962), 307–326.

crats offered another, postponing the ban on notes under $10 until 1840. This amendment was defeated fifty-seven to fifteen: the fifteen votes in favor were all Democratic. It was merely a gesture (there were only twenty-two Democrats in the lower House), but one which reflected party direction and obedience.[13]

Banking and politics in the state of Pennsylvania provide a capsule example of the problems that Washington Jacksonians would confront in their efforts to develop a political program to deal with national banking. The state was characterized by various economic divisions: the northeastern counties were heavily involved with New York City merchants while the southern and some of the western parts of the state traded with Baltimore instead of Philadelphia. The lack of economic unity accounts for the conclusion of Richard McCormick that Pennsylvania was unique among the Middle states in having an undisciplined, unorganized political structure.[14] But if important Pennsylvania economic interests found it difficult to get together in any positive way, they did agree that Jackson's opposition to a protective tariff, internal improvements, and, above all, the BUS, was a mistake.

Pennsylvania Jacksonians were weakened in the early thirties first by the defection of the Calhounites and then by Jackson's BUS veto. The veto was probably directly responsible for Jackson's reduced margin in Pennsylvania in the 1832 presidential election.[15] Even though Pennsylvania Jacksonians still had a fairly popular national leader and an attractive

13. *Niles Register*, Oct. 11, 18, 1834; Bryan, "State Banking in Maryland," 77–80; *Maryland House Journal*, Feb. 12, 14, 1835.

14. Louis Hartz, *Economic Policy and Democratic Thought: Pennsylvania, 1776–1860* (Cambridge, 1948), 9–11; McCormick, *Second American Party System*, 134.

15. Charles M. Snyder, *The Jacksonian Heritage: Pennsylvania Politics, 1833–1848* (Harrisburg, Pa., 1958), 23–27.

ideology in championing the will of the people against the aristocrats and monopolists allegedly threatening the forces of egalitarianism, the problem remained that such an ideology was not adaptable to state needs, since both parties had to respond to sectional interests and pressure groups rather than a fictitous public will. Louis Hartz's intriguing study argues that neither Democrats nor Whigs were consistently anti-bank or pro-bank, because the demands of special interests forced both parties to charter banks.[16]

Despite Hartz's consensual treatment of Pennsylvania politics and banking, there were differences, sometimes significant differences, between the Jacksonian and Whig responses to state banking. The Whig anti-Masonic coalition which swept into power in the fall of 1835 dramatically expanded state banking and resulted in a semblance of unity among Democrats around an anti-bank, anti-monopoly position. The political unity was enhanced by the reappearance of the dreaded "Monster" in the guise of a state charter, when the former national BUS became the Pennsylvania BUS. Indeed, the anti-bank Democrats were so rejuvenated by this event that more cautious and traditional Pennsylvania Democrats found it difficult to contain the anti-bank spirit within their ranks. Though they had few opportunities to translate their new political energy into action, Pennsylvania Democrats did pass an anti-bank bill in the Assembly after the Panic of 1837, only to see it killed in the Senate. Nevertheless, Democrats took credit for guarding the public against the monopolists.[17]

16. Hartz, *Economic Policy and Democratic Thought*, 23–30, 62–65, 77–79, 292–293.

17. Hartz compares the bank chartering of the 1814 legislature with the Whig-anti-Masonic bank expansion in 1835 in reaching his conclusion that both Democrats and Whigs favored bank expansion. This evidence may well support Hartz's conclusion that state pressures forced both parties to expand banking but it is misleading to

An important transition occured in Pennsylvania politics and economics when even certain economic interests began to adapt to the Democratic rhetoric. As Louis Hartz has shown, corporations easily utilized the anti-charter rhetoric and began to define themselves as individual enterprises unfairly and unjustly hindered by state regulation. Pointing to the lack of an administrative, bureaucratic system outside the political structure, Hartz argues that political parties were open to too many diverse pressures to administer such responsibilities efficiently. Consequently, the most attractive solution to the vexing problems inherent in the relationship between politics and economics lay in the direction of separation of the two.[18] Treasury Secretary Woodbury would soon learn this lesson as he labored to impose controls on the national banking structure only to find that the political pressures were too great and too contradictory and that these responsibilities were best removed from the political sphere, even if they had to be abandoned to the jurisdiction of Wall Street interests.

In the Old Northwest—Ohio, Indiana, and Illinois—nebulous political groups formed in response to the contest for the presidency in 1824, a time when the lines between national and state politics were rarely clear and often nonexistent. These spongy political organizations incorporated various loyalties and were most often guided by personal attachments and factionalism rather than by any clearly defined policy. Except for Ohio, where cohesive party organization and dis-

---

compare the actions of the 1814 legislature with those taken by a similar body at a time when the banking issue was intensely politicized (*ibid.*, 62–65; Snyder, *The Jacksonian Heritage*, 83–85, 120–121).

18. Hartz, *Economic Policy and Democratic Thought*, 77–79, 292–293.

cipline originated as early as 1828, this region operated on a "no party" basis until well into the thirties. Even then, the Whigs lagged far behind the Democrats in effective organizing.[19]

The organizations which formed in these states initiated political actions similar to those carried on in other states under more partisan direction. The relative absence of partisan politics was useful to those who wished to neutralize the potentially divisive issues of banking and internal improvements. Consequently, it was common for politicians in these states to be "Jackson men" and still oppose Washington policy on banking and related economic issues. In such a situation, enterprising Democrats who recognized and used Jackson's personal appeal while having little regard for national Democratic policy felt comfortable—until the Old Hero's retirement and Van Buren's emergence as the Democratic leader.[20]

The Van Buren issue aided those hoping to disorganize and otherwise render ineffective the Democratic party. In concentrating on personal politics in the form of Van Buren's qualifications, politicians of the Old Northwest were perpetuating the personal factionalism so long identified with this region. But opposition to Van Buren was not exclusively composed of political Machiavellians disguising their real intentions. The anti-Democratic, Whiggish tendency was to view politics from a moral perspective, and often that perspective was influenced by evaluations of personal character. Demo-

19. McCormick, *Second American Party System*, 320–322; Harry R. Stevens, *The Early Jackson Party in Ohio* (Durham, N.C., 1957), 151–153; Charles M. Thompson, "The Illinois Whigs before 1846," *University of Illinois Studies in the Social Sciences*, IV (Urbana, 1915), 9–41.

20. Theodore C. Pease, *The Frontier State, 1818–1840*, The Centennial History of Illinois, II (Chicago, 1919), 136–141; Thompson, "The Illinois Whigs," 46–47.

crats had the "best cause," Ralph Waldo Emerson observed, but insisted that the Whigs had the "best men"—the latter being more important to those of the Emersonian persuasion. The political ascendency of Van Buren in the 1830's prompted the Old Northwest Whigs to sermonize over the quality of American politics. Van Buren was the manager and fixer, the very epitome of organizational, machine politics—the style of politics that the Whigs of the region had only reluctantly adopted.[21]

It is clear that when this confusion over party identification and purpose was resolved, the anti-banking sentiment, however measured and evaluated, was concentrated in the Democratic party, in uneasy alliance, to be sure, with more moderate and pro-Bank Democrats. Whigs were more uniform than the Democrats on all economic and political issues. In Illinois, commercial-minded men were recognized as Whigs; the incipient Whig organizations claimed to be the party of business, favoring a national bank, a protective tariff, and support for internal improvements. Because of Democratic divisions over such issues, Illinois Whigs were often able to dominate legislative action concerning them in spite of being in the minority. The state bank directors, coincidentally, were almost unanimously Whigs at the time Democrats were going through their fratricidal conflict over support for Van Buren.[22]

After the Panic of 1837, Democrats in Ohio, Indiana, and Illinois recommended and sometimes passed legislation regu-

21. Pease noted that Illinois Whigs were more nativist and religious than the Jacksonians (*The Frontier State*, 260–261). On this theme see the recent article by Ronald P. Formisano, "Political Character, Antipartyism and the Second Party System," *American Quarterly* (Winter, 1969), 683–709.

22. Pease, *The Frontier State*, 256–258; Thompson, "The Illinois Whigs," 52–53.

lating banking practices. With few exceptions the banking issue was a highly partisan one in these years. While Whigs remained loyal to banks in Illinois after the Panic, Democratic anti-bank sentiment increased markedly. In Ohio, a law prohibiting low-denomination bank notes was passed by the legislature on a strict party line vote and was later repealed by a Whig majority, again along party lines. But it is best to be cautious when making generalizations about issues in the Old Northwest. In Illinois, for example, the anti-banking sentiment was virtually all in the Democratic party but with few exceptions was concentrated in the southern part of the state, while Democrats from the more prosperous northern counties favored state bank support, if not expansion.[23]

Political expediency dictated the resolution of the banking issue in the Old Northwest as it did elsewhere. It is not surprising that Democratic anti-bank sentiment increased after the Panic of 1837; after all, pet banks as well as other banks had allegedly "betrayed" the administration by suspending specie payments. It soon became firm orthodoxy for Democrats to oppose the "banking interest." When some anti-bank Democrats of the region talked about a resumption of bank war campaigns, Chicago businessmen stirred uneasily in their beds, thinking of the uncertain future; but soberer gentlemen kept their heads and were right to do so, for very little happened. For all the huffing and puffing against banks carried on by the Democrats in the Old Northwest, there was anything but a "scorched earth" policy against the banking "enemy."

Politically the Jacksonians were happiest and most united when they were hunting down the dreaded bank enemy, but once they had their adversary cornered they never knew quite what to do. During debate on the issues, anti-bank

---

23. James Roger Sharp, *The Jacksonians versus the Banks*, ch. 8.

rhetoric might ring through the legislative halls, but at voting time many Democrats could be counted on to cross the aisle and join the nearly unanimous Whig bank supporters. A number of solutions to the problem were proposed. One was to whittle the defectors from the party ranks and thus sharpen the ideology and possible effectiveness of the organization. Since banking was only a single issue, however, to build the party exclusively on this basis was quixotic. Furthermore, in times of prosperity, even the most obsessive anti-bank Democrat could overlook the enterprising and aggressive elements attracted both to the party and to banks. A second solution was to harness the anti-banking sentiment in the party and work toward guarding the public through bank regulation. But Democrats were honestly confused about what to regulate, convinced that banks might evade regulation, and uneasy over the political alliances necessary to carry out such regulation. A third and more tempting solution was to cut the banking interest adrift from its political moorings and launch an era of free banking. The issue was finally resolved in this manner in Indiana, Illinois, and Michigan in the Old Northwest, following the lead of a few older states which had earlier adopted similar policies. In 1837 the Van Buren administration supplied a federal example in the form of its own advocacy of a "divorce" between bank and state. The attraction of such a remedy was that it absolved the Democrats of responsibility for the banking interests and restored the "purity" of the political organization.

The states of Virginia and New York offer the best examples of the connection between Washington banking policy and Democratic action on the state level. The alliance between the Virginia and New York Democrats was already of historical proportion. Van Buren regarded Virginia as the leader of the South and an important source of political support for his presidential ambitions. In both states, with few exceptions, Democratic majorities had ruled the state governments. If state parties were expected to follow the leadership of Washington Jacksonians on banking, that leadership should have been reflected in state action in both Virginia and New York.[24]

Virginia banking was characterized by stability and non-expansion until the 1830's, when demands for an increase in state banking capital became irresistible. Earlier refusal to charter additional state banks had resulted in a neglect of the western areas and left banking concentrated for the most part along the eastern seaboard. Coupled with this regional conflict was the more general concern that the demise of the BUS branches in 1836 would result in a flight of capital from Virginia to neighboring states where there was greater attention to the opportunities for economic growth. There was a growing consensus in Virginia that additional banking was necessary; the question was whether to increase the capital of the existing banks, to continue the practice of branch banking, or to charter independent banks.[25] All these questions were of concern to interested parties in Virginia but to no political group did they pose greater problems than to the Virginia Democracy.

Democrats gained control of the state legislature in the

---

24. An effective two-party system operated in New York before the Bank War but developed later in Virginia. Van Buren depended upon the Richmond Junto to keep Virginia in the Democratic column and enhance his chances for the presidency (McCormick, *Second American Party System*, 112–124, 184–189; Robert V. Remini, *The Election of Andrew Jackson* [Philadelphia, 1963], 53–61).

25. Virginia *House Journal*, 1834–1835, Document no. 23, contains the replies of state bankers and businessmen to the enquiries of a legislative committee on banking.

spring elections of 1835, but only by a slight majority. As the legislature convened in December, Thomas Ritchie, through the pages of the Richmond *Enquirer*, lectured his fellow Democrats on the evils of banking. His editorial entitled "Banks! Banks!" warned of the dangerous bank expansion taking place in other states; Ritchie's remedy for this problem in Virginia, however, was merely to ban note issues below $10 denomination.[26]

The Democratic legislature early the next year addressed itself to the state's banking problems by bringing in a bill for four new banks with the right to establish branches, as well as a capital increase for existing banks, then dutifully prohibited all notes below $10 denomination. Such a program would apparently satisfy everyone: the banking capital of the state was doubled (from $6.5 million to over $13 million), new bank charters were granted to both the western and seaboard areas of the state, the existing bank capitals were increased, and small-denomination bank notes were proscribed.[27] Dramatic banking expansion and mild currency reform was the legislature's formula for success.

Thomas Ritchie was not satisfied, however. He attacked the bill as constituting too great an expansion of the state's banking facilities. Democrats should not object to a "reasonable addition" but to double the banking capital was too dangerous, he warned. Enough Virginia Democrats shared Ritchie's concern to have the banking bill amended. At length, however, the entire bill was lost because no compromise could

---

26. H. H. Simms, *The Rise of the Whigs in Virginia, 1824–1840* (Richmond, 1929), 98. Thomas Ritchie was elected printer by a vote of 76 to 75 (Richmond *Enquirer*, Dec. 10, 1835). For Ritchie's anti-bank editorial see the *Enquirer* for Dec. 23, 1835.

27. *Ibid.*, Feb. 27, 1836.

be reached, and the legislature adjourned without increasing the state's banking facilities.[28]

The next session of the Virginia legislature again agreed on increases in the state's banking capital coupled with restrictions on bank practices. Expansion in adjoining states had increased the demand for additional facilities in Virginia, so that a banking bill passed with little opposition. Ritchie carefully watched the progress of the bill, again warning of the twin dangers of excessive banking capital and small-denomination bank notes. Originally reported with only a $5 note ban, the final bill contained a $10 ban, at Ritchie's urging, and a requirement that banks maintain a five to one ratio between note circulation and specie.[29]

For the most part, Virginia Jacksonians were either the outright opponents of banking or the advocates of banking regulation; disagreement between the two groups was responsible for delaying state banking expansion until 1837. Uncompromising anti-bank Jacksonians had the easiest solution to the problem, but an increasingly unrealistic one. Jacksonians who advocated regulation of banking were often confused about what to regulate and how. Still, most Democrats favored some means of insuring the public against the dangers of overbanking, as their overwhelming vote in favor of prohibiting notes under $10 indicates.[30]

28. *Ibid.* Alexander Brown wrote to William C. Rives when the Virginia bank bill was first reported, "I would not object to a moderate increase of capital, with proper restrictions, but I cannot agree to this wholesale kind of business; it is much safer to have too little banking capital than too much" (Feb. 17, 1836, Rives Papers). For the changes in the banking bill and its final defeat in the legislature see the Richmond *Enquirer*, March 12, 15, 17, 1836.

29. *Ibid.*, Dec. 20, 24, 1836; Jan. 14, March 28, 1837.

30. Democrats voted 63 to 5 in favor of the small note ban while the Whigs opposed it 42 to 6 (*Virginia House Journal*, 1836, 132).

A more important regulatory feature of the 1836 bank bill was the imposed specie ratio. The bill as passed required that only a bank's circulation (and not its deposits as well) be backed by a specie reserve, indicating how imperfectly lawmakers understood bank liabilities. One Democratic legislator proposed an amendment extending the specie ratio to deposits. The amendment, supported on a two-to-one basis by Democrats and overwhelmingly opposed by Whigs, was defeated.[31] The vote is not indicative of more economic sophistication among Virginia Democrats than among Whigs since there is no evidence that one political party understood bank liquidity better than the other. The vote does reflect a temporary alliance between the anti-bank Democrats and those advocating regulation of banks in the public interest. Jacksonian anti-bank impulses in Virginia were tentatively satisfied by the effort to impose specie reserve requirements, the advocacy of greater bank specie being tantamount to an anti-banking position.

The preceding analysis of Virginia banking and politics indicates that Jacksonian ambiguity over hard money was evolving into legislative demands that banks be strictly regulated with regard to specie holdings. But the political skills required to bring together anti-bank Democrats with those favoring specie regulation were great indeed. The same will be found true of New York, as conditions in the aftermath of the Bank War there are examined in the next, and final, state analysis.

As a result of the passage of the Safety Fund Act of 1829, New York Democrats were associated in the public mind with state banking. Most Democrats took pride in having originated this progressive piece of state legislation, but many party

---

31. Virginia Democrats supported the amendment by a 40 to 19 vote while the Whigs opposed the amendment 34 to 4 (*ibid.*, 129).

leaders were sensitive to charges of political collusion with the state's banking interests. Jacksonians therefore labored to promote a public image of independence from bankers. Van Buren wrote to Jackson in the fall of 1834 with a note of pride, "Our State Banks have been as active against us as any other interest." And yet, as Van Buren explained in the same letter, New York Whigs alleged that the Democrats were the pro-bank party in the state. The Albany *Argus* answered such charges in October 1834 by publishing a list of the more than seventy banks in New York and from this list identifying only five New York City and nineteen upstate banks as Democratic; the remainder were designated as Whig-controlled or as having no political affiliation.[32] The *Argus'* modest claim that only twenty-four of the more than seventy banks in the state could be called "Democratic" was designed to disprove the allegation that Democrats controlled the state banks.

Faithful New York Jacksonians labored to improve their anti-bank credentials by opposing an expansion of state banking. During the 1833–1834 State legislative session, John A. Dix wrote to Silas Wright in Washington that New York Jacksonians were "denouncing all monsters in a moneyed shape, whether predicated by federal or state authority," and the faithful Azariah Flagg jubilantly reported to Wright that the last three days of the state legislature "have been distinguished by the death of 30 Bank applications."[33]

However, at the end of the legislative session which Flagg, Dix, and others had praised for its strong anti-bank actions, the ever watchful New York *Evening Post* noted that eight new banks had been chartered. It called upon the *Argus* and

32. Van Buren to Jackson, Oct. 18, 1834, Van Buren Papers; Albany *Argus*, Oct. 18, 1834.

33. Dix to Wright, Feb. 11, 1834; Flagg to Wright, Feb. 14, 1834. Azariah C. Flagg Papers, New York Public Library.

Albany Regency to "extend its opposition to our whole rotten and appressive banking system" by coming out in favor of free banking, which it claimed to be the only proper position.[34] The state's leading Democrats were caught between the extremes of those pushing for a large increase in state-chartered banks and the emerging "Loco-foco" position advocated by the *Evening Post*, which urged the state legislature to free the banking business altogether. The *Argus* answered the *Post* and other critics by stating that it was on record as opposing small denomination bank notes and excessive state bank chartering, and favoring further restrictions on banking operations. The *Argus* defended the Safety Fund system and other legislative action as necessary means to achieve these ends, and demanded to know why, if banking were as bad as the *Post* claimed, it should then be thrown open to everyone.[35]

Despite the *Argus'* logic, the Democrats, by opposing a dramatic expansion of state banking, did lend support to their critics' claim that they were overly protective of existing banks. Thurlow Weed's Albany *Evening Journal*, a leading Whig press, turned the Jacksonian rhetoric back upon state Democrats by charging that their favoritism toward state banks supported an economic monopoly which helped a few at the expense of the many.[36] While they might agree on little else, Thurlow Weed's Albany *Evening Journal* and William Leggett's *Evening Post* shared the view that New York Democratic banking policy required modification. Theodore Sedgwick assured Van Buren that the solution lay in Democratic support for free banking: "I incline to believe that this anti-monopoly warfare will extend—and if it does extend, I cannot imagine that there can be a doubt of the issue in favor

34. New York *Evening Post*, May 8, 1834.
35. Albany *Argus*, Oct. 18, Dec. 22, 1834, Jan. 5, 1835.
36. Albany *Evening Journal*, Nov. 18, 1834.

of those who contend for an overthrow of the present system of Corporations."[37]

In spite of attacks by the anti-bank *Evening Post* and the anti-Democratic *Evening Journal,* the state's leading Democrats were determined to maintain their support for legislative regulation of state banks. Influential Democrats like Azariah Flagg were confident that state regulation could eliminate most of the evils of banking, and the number of banks could be kept to a necessary minimum by legislative caution.[38] Few Democrats were willing to have the legislature abandon its responsibilities toward banks in preference for a policy of free banking, which most of them interpreted as an opportunity for anyone to set up a bank and issue notes without limit. "The repeal of the restraining law has no advocates," Van Buren's son reported to his father in January 1835. But what lay ahead? "I don't see what else is to be done hereafter but increase the number of Banks with judgment and moderation. Leggett has helped the Monopolist more than any Editor in the Union by his indiscreet course."[39]

The younger Van Buren stated correctly the New York Democrats' dilemma regarding state banking. By limiting state bank chartering, Democrats were either directly or indirectly protecting the interests of existing banks. But increasing the number of banks with "judgment and moderation" meant that the greater one's influence in the Democratic party, the better one's chances of obtaining a coveted bank charter. "I do not say what will be done," Churchill C. Cambreleng wrote to Van Buren, "as long as the legislators can make money by the charters of their own creation or prominent

37. Sedgwick to Van Buren, Dec. 29, 1834, Van Buren Papers.
38. Flagg to N. P. Tallmadge, Feb. 6, 1835, Tallmadge Papers.
39. John Van Buren to Van Buren, Jan. 14, 1835, Van Buren Papers.

men can get the salaries of President and cashiers by enlisting in the ranks of the democracy."[40]

The Democratic formula for state banking was unsatisfactory to those who wanted a rapidly accelerated economy; but every additional bank chartered was regarded by Flagg and other New York Jacksonians as a deviation from Democratic principles. Flagg and others had been able to exert enough influence on the 1835 legislature to hold down banking expansion in the state. In the next session, the Democrats were increasingly criticized by the Whigs in general and by the New York *Journal of Commerce* in particular on the grounds that the party was hindering the economic progress of New York. The *Journal of Commerce* called upon the new Democratic legislature to charter every bank requested and to increase the capital of existing banks. The paper attacked the Democrats for pursuing a "restrictive policy in relation to banking facilities," and described in these terms New York's economic potential, should the Democrats reverse their policy: "Keep off the bandages from the infant Hercules —give him the free use of his limbs, and he will become a giant."[41]

The Democratic position on banking was difficult politically, endeavoring to occupy the middle ground between those who favored an unlimited expansion of state banking and those who opposed all banks. A lack of heroic or even stirring rhetoric to articulate their position added to the Democrats' discomfort. The official party line on banking was typified by the Richmond *Enquirer*'s call for a "careful and reasonable addition to the banking capital." The Albany *Argus* exhorted the New York faithful to "labor to relieve our banking system of its defects, whilst we preserve, as far as consistent with

40. Cambreleng to Van Buren, Nov. 2, 1835, *ibid.*
41. New York *Journal of Commerce*, Oct. 30, Nov. 28, 1835.

sound policy and the popular voice, its manifest advantages."[42] David Campbell, the Democratic Governor of Virginia, described the Democratic state banking policy succinctly: "We want some additional banking capital—but not much."[43] Sensible as this position may have been, it scarcely equalled the heroic battle cries of a few years earlier when Democrats led the people's struggle against the "Monster." Now the party was asking the same people to cooperate with the lesser enemy and to work for reforms. The New York *Evening Post*, in attacking all banks as well as their Democratic supporters, simply lowered its sights from national to state "monsters." Amid the confusion, more and more Democrats cautiously moved toward advocating the separation of government and banking.

Firm conclusions regarding state politics and banking must await more exhaustive studies; however, certain theories can be formulated based on these selective analyses. State Democrats were more divided over banking and hard-money issues than was the opposition. As a party they were not consistently or clearly in favor of hard-money and anti-bank measures, but a majority tended to move in this direction, and only a minority (in many cases a very small one) opposed them. By contrast, the Whiggish opposition was more unanimous in its support for the agencies of credit and prosperity. Therefore, the failure to check bank expansion and impose meaningful banking regulation at the state level was not due so much to ideological divisions among Jacksonians as to the fact that such actions were defeated by a united Whig opposition.

42. Richmond *Enquirer*, Dec. 10, 1835; Albany *Argus*, quoted in New York *Evening Post*, Dec. 2, 1834.
43. D. Campbell to nephew, Jan. 10, 1836, Campbell Papers.

5

Pet Banks and
Congressional Politics

The difficulties involved in regulating banking through state action pressured Jacksonians to develop a national banking program. How the Democrats met or evaded this challenge can best be evaluated through an analysis of congressional action during the pet banking era (from 1834 through the passage of the Deposit-Distribution Act in 1836). We shall limit ourselves in this chapter to legislative proposals on banking and currency in the Twenty-third and Twenty-fourth Congresses. It seems a fair assumption, however, that these votes represented general economic-political attitudes in Congress. Furthermore, it is a fundamental premise of this analysis that Treasury policy in general and pet bank management in particular were influenced and ultimately determined by congressional action. It is therefore important to understand the political makeup of Congress and how it defined and limited the administration's alternatives.

The Washington *Globe* rigidly defined the political choices open to congressmen convening in December 1833 for the Twenty-third Congress. Although Jackson's victory over the BUS was now linked with the more divisive issues of deposit removal and the governmental use of state banks, Frank Blair in his editorials argued that the only issue confronting Congress was the threat of BUS recharter. Deposit removal and state bank use were secondary but definitely connected with the larger question of a national bank, and, Blair insisted, an attack on any part of the executive program raised the dangerous possibility of the "Monster's" recharter.[1] Blair's political formula for Democratic identification consisted of equating BUS opposition with Jacksonianism; the Washington editor was therefore confident of a Democratic majority in the House. The fall elections increased his confidence, and he predicted that the new House would contain 147 Jacksonians out of a total of 239. When Andrew Stevenson, a Virginia Democrat, received 142 first-ballot votes for House Speaker, Blair assured the party faithful that the Jacksonians commanded a workable House majority.[2]

An understanding of congressional political loyalties during the Jacksonian era requires examination beyond Blair's simplistic analysis. Hezekiah Niles more accurately forecast the complex political nature of the Twenty-third Congress when he predicted that it would contain six distinct political groups, despite efforts to divide Congress into pro- and anti-Jackson parties. "And there will be divisions, perhaps, among each of these as to leading matters about to be presented," Niles concluded.[3] The political confusion in Congress was the result of varied electoral practices on the local level. Many candidates for Congress relied upon their names and prestige or incum-

1. Washington *Globe*, Nov. 28, 1833.
2. *Ibid.*, Aug. 29, Nov. 8, Dec. 3, 1833.
3. Niles identified the six groups as "the Jackson Party, proper; the Jackson-Van Buren Party; the Jackson-anti Van Buren Party; the Anti-Jackson Party; the Nullifying and Anti-Jackson Party; the Anti Masonic and Anti-Jackson Party" (*Niles Register*, Dec. 7, 1833).

bent position as credentials for the office, rather than offering the voters a political identification. Contributing to this practice was the persistence of the Jeffersonian tradition that men in public life should act independently and not follow slavishly the dictates of any political persuasion or organization. Many candidates, accordingly, proudly identified themselves as "Independents." Moreover, before the 1834 Whig movement, without the discipline prompted by an organized opposition, the Jacksonians were loosely grouped into various state cliques called "Friends of Jackson." Thus on some roll calls there were "Independents" who supported Jackson while some "Jackson men" opposed the administration.

The lack of rigorous political discipline makes it difficult to establish with statistical certainty the dimensions of the Jacksonian political movement. *Ex post facto* political identifications are sometimes necessary for the purpose of making quantifying judgments about congressional action. Despite the early political uncertainty and later intense partisanship of the 1830's, much influential writing about this period begins with the premise that Jacksonian Democracy thoroughly commanded American politics. Previous accounts of this era have asserted that the Jacksonians were political wizards in accomplishing their goals and, conversely, that inaction on certain issues was also deliberate.[4] Some precise evidence regarding party strength is necessary to modify these impressions.

4. Arthur Schlesinger, Jr., in the *Age of Jackson* emphasizes the political conflict of the era but argues that Jackson represented the "people" and that the opposition business community had unusual leverage on the political machinery. Bray Hammond's *Banks and Politics* attacks Schlesinger's thesis but not his premise that Jacksonian Democrats represented the public will. In Hammond's view, the Jacksonians were eminently successful: "What the Jacksonians decided on, they directed their propaganda toward, and got" (326). The index of *Banks and Politics* cites the "Whigs" once (771).

Jackson's political strength in Congress was nominally greater before he undertook the executive actions with which his presidency is so prominently identified: the Bank veto and deposit removal.[5] Perhaps these actions did not directly cause the reduced Jacksonian majorities in Congress, but many Democrats made that connection and were keenly aware that the Bank War's political casualties endangered legislation affecting banking and currency. The exact number of defections from Jacksonian ranks over these issues depends upon a firm political identification of Jacksonians before the emergence of the Whigs in 1834, which, for reasons already mentioned, is no easy task.

In establishing political identity, both administration and opposition sources have been used in the present study, noting that each side tended to exaggerate the extent of its political following. In many cases, *Niles Register* has proven a valuable and objective source, although Niles was reluctant to identify individual congressmen by party. If anything, this study has been liberal in Democratic identifications. If Frank Blair's *Globe* claimed a congressman as a Democrat, that definition has been accepted, keeping in mind that in times of intense political conflict party leaders are often guilty of wishful thinking. Upon finding that a congressman presented himself to the voters as a "Jackson man," that self-description has been accepted. Rigidly to limit Democrats to those who voted with the administration on crucial roll calls would de-

5. Although imprecise, standard studies of the House cite the relative decline in Jacksonian congressional strength: George B. Galloway, *History of the House of Representatives* (New York, 1961), 296; Alexander S. De Alva, *History and Procedure of the House of Representatives* (Cambridge, 1916), 411. For a recent treatment which points out the political cost to Democrats of the Bank War see Robert V. Remini, *Andrew Jackson and the Bank War* (New York, 1967).

feat the purpose of measuring the extent and significance of Jacksonian defections over banking and currency policy.

The first meaningful test of congressional response to the administration's banking policy came on a series of resolutions reported by the House Ways and Means Committee in April 1834. The first resolution opposed BUS recharter and carried by a vote of 134 to 82. The second resolution opposed the restoration of the public money to the Bank and tested Blair's strategy of subordinating all related economic issues to BUS recharter. The House approved the administration-sponsored resolution but by the much narrower margin of 118 to 103. A third resolution approving the use of state banks as federal depositories passed by a vote of 117 to 105.[6] It was southern defections which reduced the pro-administration majority on the last two resolutions.

Of the sixty-two southern congressmen, forty-one had been elected as "Jackson men." The administration collected thirty-nine southern votes against BUS recharter, but only twenty-two each on the resolution against replacing the public money in the BUS and the one favoring use of state banks as depositories. The most serious defection occurred within the Virginia delegation, where thirteen pro-administration votes on recharter fell to six each over deposit removal and the use of state banks.

The administration could not afford further defections among its southern supporters. Sectional imbalance within the Jacksonian coalition increased anxieties over disunion, and the dwindling Jacksonian majority also increased the difficulty of passing desired congressional legislation. Sensitivities regarding executive power allegedly caused southerners to withdraw their support for Jackson's unprecedented action

6. *House Journal*, 23 Cong., 1 sess., 483–487.

toward the national Bank. The administration's answer was to encourage congressional regulation of pet banks. The administration hoped that such legislation would neutralize southern fears about the arbitrary exercise of executive power. Those congressmen truly concerned about the exercise of presidential power over the public money were invited by the *Globe* to "bind up the Executive by laws so strict that abuse cannot find a loophole."[7]

The administration's bill to regulate pet banks was more than a political gesture to coax errant southerners back to the party; it was the first official statement of the administration's program for currency reform. Secretary Taney's report to the Ways and Means Committee in April 1834 had formed the basis for the Democratic bill. Taney argued that reform must attack the great amount of bank notes in circulation. "The great evil of our present currency is, the disproportion between the paper in circulation and the coin prepared to redeem it," the secretary stated. He insisted that the existence of a national bank frustrated the removal of bank paper since states were unwilling to limit state bank note issues and allow the national bank to monopolize this practice. He assured the administration's critics that Jacksonians would neither abandon state banks nor abolish all paper money, but argued that greater amounts of gold and silver were needed in circulation and competing bank notes of low denomination must be removed.[8]

James K. Polk, chairman of the House Ways and Means Committee, promptly reported a bill following Taney's suggestions. The Polk-sponsored bill required government receivers after March 1836 to stop receiving the paper money of any bank that continued to issue bank notes of denomina-

7. Washington *Globe*, April 29, 1834.
8. *Register of Debates*, 23 Cong., 1 sess., Appendix, 157–161.

tions under $5. Both Taney and Polk recommended a gradual approach but made clear the administration's intention to raise the prohibition to $20 in the future. The effectiveness of the legislation depended upon the desire of banks to have their paper received by the government. The bill's other provisions dealt with the concern over executive power. The Secretary of the Treasury would continue to select the state banks used by the government but could not discontinue the services of any bank, a prerogative reserved for Congress.[9]

The House passed the administration's pet banks bill late in the session by a vote of 112 to 90.[10] The voting pattern was similar to that on the resolutions favoring removal and the use of state banks; strategy designed to allay southern fears proved unsuccessful, since only twenty southerners supported the administration on this roll call. In addition, half a dozen western votes were lost through abstentions, but in the New England and Middle states Democrats demonstrated greater loyalty. The bill was lost through the Senate's refusal to consider the House bill. Such an event was not unexpected, and may have been part of the Democratic strategy to blame the Senate's inaction for any subsequent financial disruption.[11]

The southern defections from the Jacksonian crusade as the Bank War continued appeared more serious than they actually were in terms of an intraparty struggle. Many of the southerners who were anti-BUS but equally opposed to removal and pet banking used these issues, either sincerely or otherwise, as their opportunity to move into the Whig ranks. Jacksonians could then dismiss them as part of the Bank "aristocracy," a situation more acceptable than their presence

9. *Ibid.*, 4602–4622.

10. *House Journal*, 23 Cong., 1 sess., 824–829.

11. Congressman Richard Wilde made this point during House debate (*Register of Debates*, 23 Cong., 1 sess., 4632–4640.)

within the Democratic party.[12] Southerners who scurried over to the Whig side during the first session of the Twenty-third Congress were not hard-money radicals disgusted over the administration's use of state banks. Despite southern rhetoric about hard money, these defecting congressmen, with the exception of William F. Gordon, did not rejoin the administration when its anti-bank posture stiffened in the controversy over the independent treasury.

The possibility that defections among southern congressmen were caused by opposition to Van Buren's rise within the party is more difficult to assess. Pet banking from its inception had been identified with New York interests and therefore with the presidential ambitions of the vice-president. One way to attack Van Buren indirectly and challenge "grasping" northern commercial interests as well was for southerners to attack the pet banking structure which allegedly gave the New Yorker so much of his political power. The Empire State's alleged dominance of pet banking operations and Van Buren's imminent command of the Democratic party coincided with increasing southern anxiety about the slavery issue. Jacksonian defectors were quick to link all these points

12. An example is Blair's treatment of the Virginia delegation. After the 1833 congressional election, Blair claimed that the Virginia delegation was comprised of sixteen Democrats and five opposition men, calculated by using BUS opposition as the test of party identification. Only seven of the sixteen so identified as Democrats subsequently supported the administration in the twenty-third Congress; accordingly, Blair dubbed the other nine as opposition men. He could then consider the 1835 Virginia congressional election a triumph of Jacksonian Democracy by contrasting the results of this election with his revised figures on the 1833 elections. The seven Jackson men of the 1833 elections swelled to 15 as a result of the 1835 election, whereas by using Blair's pre-revisionist political identifications, the result from 1833 to 1835 was a net loss of one Jacksonian congressman in the Virginia delegation (Washington *Globe*, Aug. 29, 1833, May 19, 1835; Richmond *Enquirer*, May 13, 1835).

together in justifying their opposition to administration policy; pet bank patronage, unscrupulous Regency politics, and fanatic abolitionism were all said to have their peculiar home in New York.[13]

Jacksonians had little to show for their efforts during the first session of the Twenty-third Congress. Although the administration's policies had not been reversed, they had received only precarious political support at best. Furthermore, the Jacksonian sincerity regarding currency reform had been challenged vigorously by southern critics of pet banking. Jacksonians attempted to refurbish their image as champions of hard money near the end of the session with the passage of the Coinage Act. This Act, establishing a ratio of sixteen to one between gold and silver (a deliberate overevaluation of gold in order to encourage its coinage) had been substituted for a carefully drawn bill providing for a subsidiary coinage using a truer ratio between gold and silver. In June 1834 the original proposal was hastily withdrawn by Campbell P. White, a New York City Jacksonian, and the bill imposing a sixteen to one ratio substituted.[14] Through this legislation, the Jacksonians were hoping more for political rewards than for financial effectiveness.

Blair admitted that the "theoretical proportion" between gold and silver was less than sixteen to one, but that the "practical proportion" was greater because "The People want a gold currency"—an interesting example of intricate financial adjustment through public opinion. Blair predicted that the opposition would vote against the legislation because the

13. McCormick, *The Second American Party System*, 250, 338–340, evaluates the impact of Van Buren's candidacy upon southern politics.

14. Paul M. O'Leary, "The Coinage Legislation of 1834," *Journal of Political Economy*, XLV (Feb. 1937), 80–94.

circulation of gold was against the interests of the national Bank.[15] But the political value of the Coinage Act to Jacksonians was undercut when enough Whigs voted for the bill to make it a bipartisan measure.[16] Blair explained the Whig conversion on the grounds that public opinion forced them to vote for the bill against their true interests. He reminded the Whigs that the legislation "is a measure of deadly hostility to the interests of the Bank, will supersede its notes, and is the harbinger of a *real* sound currency."[17] It seemed as though the opposition refused to play fair with the issues Blair and other Jacksonian tacticians had chosen for disagreement. The administration would be forced to escalate its hard-money efforts in order to draw cleanly the distinctions between Jacksonians and the "Bank Party."

Various circumstances favored the chances for congressional approval of a pet banks bill by the second session of the Twenty-third Congress. The administration's failure to secure a bank regulation bill from the first session was more than matched by the opposition's failure to reverse executive action. By the time the second or short session convened in December 1834, the pet banks system had been operating for over a year. Roger Taney had been replaced by Levi Woodbury, a secondary and less controversial figure in the Bank War. Furthermore, the Whigs seemed resolved to abandon their politically suicidal course of BUS recharter.

Polk reintroduced the administration's bill and debate began in February 1835. The proposal contained a significant change in that it required pet banks to hold a one-fourth

15. Washington *Globe*, June 14, 1834.
16. O'Leary, "Coinage Legislation," 90–91.
17. Washington *Globe*, June 14, 1834.

specie reserve against circulation.[18] The administration had concentrated upon removing low-denomination bank notes from circulation, but the specie reserve clause marked the first sign of a shift in administrative thinking from currency reform to some form of bank regulation through legislation. Bank notes were not a bank's only liability (the administration was to be rudely reminded of this fact by its more financially astute congressional foes) but they were its greatest single liability, and the insertion of the clause in the bill reflects the administration's increased concern over unregulated pet banking operations.

Polk's speech in defense of the bill did not emphasize the specie reserve clause, since such emphasis might lend support to the argument that state banks were unreliable institutions for holding the public money. Assuring the House that the administration had great confidence in the reliability and usefulness of state banks, Polk skillfully portrayed the pet banks as a reliable alternative to a national bank and defended them against some southerners urging the discontinued use of all banks by the government.[19]

The most ominous warning to the administration concerning plans for banking legislation and monetary reform was the increasing demand in Congress that the benefits of pet banking be dispersed more widely. In the opinion of most congressmen, the significance of the administration's pet banks system was that it necessarily involved financial rewards for certain state institutions. Congress was willing to share the administration's responsibility for managing the public money but only on the condition that no state bank have special privileges. In a society which advocated "equal rights," it was difficult

18. *Register of Debates*, 23 Cong., 2 sess., 1266–1281.
19. *Ibid.*

for even the staunchest administration supporter to resist these egalitarian appeals.

The congressional restlessness further manifested itself in demands for pet banks to pay an interest charge for the public deposits. Woodbury himself had unwittingly raised this point in his annual report to Congress by suggesting that in case of an unusual surplus in the Treasury an interest charge might be levied or the funds temporarily invested in state stocks.[20] The reference to interest payments was unfortunate politically because it seemed to admit the inherent injustice of the government policy which benefited a few banks at the expense of the public.

Polk and Woodbury conferred on how to meet the new challenge: "This is a point that will probably be much insisted upon by the opponents of the bill," Polk warned the secretary. Woodbury was in complete agreement. He assured Polk that the charging of interest would force the more reliable pets to give up the deposits, endanger the entire system, and pave the way for the recharter of a national bank.[21] Polk solemnly passed these warnings on to his colleagues, adding that the BUS had never paid interest when it held the federal funds. The Speaker urged in characteristic Jacksonian fashion that congressional labors should be directed toward reducing government revenue rather than augmenting it. Polk cleared up the apparent administration inconsistency about interest payments by explaining that Woodbury's recommendation presupposed a large Treasury balance. He noted, too, that a guarantee to the banks that they be allowed the use of the

---

20. *Ibid.*, Appendix, 61–62.

21. "Mr. Polks Minutes, 2 Feb. 1835," United States Treasury Department Records, Communications from Committees, Senate and House, National Archives; Woodbury to Polk, Feb. 26, 28, 1835, Polk Papers.

money for a specified time would also be necessary under such conditions.[22]

The arguments by Polk and other House leaders were successful in holding the administration's majority in line and protecting the pet banks from the twin threats of an interest charge and a general distribution of the public money, but an amendment to the administration's bill offered by the pro-Bank Horace Binney clearly exposed the difficulties of securing satisfactory legislation. Binney's amendment proposed that the administration's one-fourth specie reserve clause be extended to cover a bank's deposits as well as its note circulation.[23] The Binney amendment was sound in theory, since deposits as well as note circulation constitute a bank's liability, and the proposal is interesting because it represents one of the earliest attempts to regulate the relationship between the two by legislation. But the amendment would have been unduly punitive in practice. The administration's bill would have allowed a bank's specie reserve to be deposited in other banks and would have encouraged the concentration of specie along the eastern seaboard. Binney's amendment would require each bank to hold in its own vault the legal minimum of specie, working the greatest hardship upon western pet banks. In the eastern cities where interbank exchanges were frequent such an arrangement would have been feasible, but western bank deposits were largely composed of paper money derived from land sales. Western pets could neither frequently nor rapidly exchange these notes for specie from the various banks which issued them, yet while these exchanges were carried on, which might take months, they would be required to hold sufficient specie as a reserve against the deposits shown on their books.

Before these arguments were presented to the House, the

22. *Register of Debates*, 23 Cong., 2 sess., 1266–1281.
23. *House Journal*, 23 Cong., 2 sess., 370–371.

Binney amendment was put to a vote, after the ratio had been changed to one-fifth, and passed by a vote of 109 to 99.[24]

The administration was now in the most serious difficulty. It had urged Congress to pass legislation regulating the deposit banks, and the House, under a Democratic majority, had done so. Reuben Whitney, anxiously watching the House proceedings, lamented to Lewis after the passage of the Binney amendment, "The misfortune is, that but few of our friends understand the subject. I wish I could be pinned to Polk's back as his prompter."[25] But Whitney's explanation does not account for the breakdown of the Democratic majority over the Binney proposal. Twenty-eight pro-administration congressmen voted for the Binney amendment. By far the largest number out of this group of Democratic defectors were the administration's "friends," so called through Blair's generosity, since most of them had uneven records of Democratic loyalty during the preceding session of the Twenty-third Congress. These men were not confused, as Whitney believed, but by their votes demonstrated their displeasure over the administration's pet banks system by saddling it with punitive restrictions. Most of the Democratic pro-Binney amendment votes came from the South: ten from Virginia and five from Georgia. These anti-bank Democrats refused to sanction Jackson's deposit removal and the administration's use of state banks as fiscal agents. A much smaller group—seven congressmen—reversed their votes and supported Polk's call for a reconsideration of the Binney amendment. Having honestly misunderstood the implications of the amendment

24. *Register of Debates*, 23 Cong., 2 sess., 1437–1441, 1443. A Georgia Congressman offered an amendment which would have excluded the money received from land sales from the Binney specie ratio but it was rejected without a division (*House Journal*, 23 Cong., 2 sess., 421).

25. Whitney to Lewis, Feb. 16, 1835, Lewis-Neilson Papers.

they were persuaded by explanations by Polk and others that it would be disruptive to the pet banks system. The remainder of Democratic votes for the Binney amendment can be explained by fuzzy party identification. Some congressmen, still hopefully listed by Blair and others as Democrats, were establishing through their votes their identity with the Whig organization.[26]

Senate actions on pet banking legislation reveal Democratic divisions similar to those in the House. A Senate bill reported by a select committee on executive patronage was introduced by John C. Calhoun in 1835. The bill required an interest charge on the deposits in pet banks but left the exact amount unspecified. Two per cent was agreed upon, although there were complaints that this would work a hardship on southwestern banks. Few senators were willing to shield the pets from an interest charge, despite the many arguments about its adverse effect upon pet banking operations.[27]

Daniel Webster introduced a Senate amendment similar to Binney's in the House, calling for a specie reserve against bank deposits and circulation. The ratio was left unspecified, but Thomas Benton, in his zeal to prove that he was no friend of banks, proposed a ratio of one to four, even more restrictive than the final version of the House amendment. It was put to a vote and narrowly defeated, nineteen to seventeen. Webster proposed a one to five ratio which was adopted by a vote of twenty-seven to six; all negative votes were Democratic.[28]

The debate on Binney's amendment in the House had little effect on Senate Democrats. The arguments of Polk, Cambreleng, and other House Jacksonians were certainly known

26. *House Journal*, 23 Cong., 2 sess., 373–374, 420–421.
27. *Senate Journal*, 23 Cong., 2 sess., 148, 193; *Register of Debates*, 23 Cong., 2 sess., 620–621, 630.
28. *Senate Journal*, 23 Cong., 2 sess., 197.

to Senate Democrats, yet the Webster amendment carried in the Senate with strong Democratic support. The Senate Whigs either voted for the amendment or abstained, which should have made it clear to Senate Jacksonians that the amendment was unfavorable to the administration's pet banking system. Benton, in supporting the specie reserve ratio, carried along such loyal Jacksonians as Lewis Linn of Missouri, John Robinson of Illinois, James Buchanan of Pennsylvania, and Alfred Cuthbert of Georgia. On the other hand, Silas Wright, the administration's Senate leader, in opposing the bill found himself in the company of Senators Nathaniel Tallmadge, John Tipton, and John Ruggles, who would all emerge as Conservatives over the issue of the independent treasury.[29] The division in the ranks of Senate Democrats was not a polarization into hard-money and business wings of the party. Benton declared during Senate debate over the interest charge for the federal deposits that he was in favor of "making the banks pay for establishing a hard money currency,"[30] but his Democratic colleagues on these roll calls did not share the Missouri senator's enthusiasm for hard money.

The actions of the upper house reveal that Senate Jacksonians were plagued by the same political dilemma as frustrated administration supporters in the lower house. Pet banking required an embarrassing association between Democrats and the interests of a few banks; because of this, an increasing number of Democrats enthusiastically seized upon opportunities to prove their loyalty to the Jacksonian cause by supporting legislation which promised banking restrictions and was therefore vaguely against the banking interest.

Polk, recognizing the unreliability of the House Democratic majority, kept both Senate and House bills in committee

29. *Ibid.*, 199.
30. *Congressional Globe*, 23 Cong., 2 sess., 296.

rather than risk the passage of an unworkable regulation bill. Such a turn of events was perfectly satisfactory to Reuben Whitney, whose letters to the Girard Bank's William Lewis continued to inflate his role as Washington protector of the banking interests. Prior to the opening of Congress, Whitney had warned Lewis of increasing hostility toward all banks, assuring him, however, that no legislation regulating pet banks would be introduced by the administration. While the bill was being debated, Whitney egotistically gave Lewis his assurance that he would see to it that any legislation adversely affecting the pets did not pass. At the close of the session Whitney was jubilant, taking credit for the bill's failure, although he again warned Lewis of anti-banking sentiment among Jacksonians.[31]

The Democratic dilemma created by the attraction of anti-bank rhetoric on one hand, and the responsibility for managing and protecting the pet banks on the other, explains Jacksonian ambivalence toward early attempts to separate the government from all banking. Congressional efforts to implement some type of independent treasury operations paralleled the administration's endeavors to secure a pet bank regulation bill in the Twenty-third Congress. The advocates of an independent treasury challenged the administration's sincerity about hard money and attacked pet banking operations as being discriminatory. Such charges not only embarrassed administration Democrats; what was worse, these independent treasury proposals originated with southern Calhounites, not a welcome source of Jacksonian inspiration.

During the first session of the Twenty-third Congress, the Virginia Calhounite, William F. Gordon, had offered an amendment to the administration's pet banks regulation bill

31. Whitney to Lewis, Nov. 6, 1834, Feb. 16, 23, March 1, 4, 1835, Lewis-Neilson Papers.

prohibiting government use of any banks and requiring the public money to be kept in the Treasury vaults. House Democrats prevented the amendment from becoming anything more than a political gesture, since debate dealt with the alternatives of a national bank and the use of state banks.[32] In his Treasury report to the next session, however, Secretary Woodbury accepted the principle of an independent treasury should pet banking prove unworkable. Woodbury's gratuitous recognition of the Gordon proposal was probably meant to inform the Whig coalition that their attacks on Treasury policy would not lead to the rechartering of a national bank. At the same time, Woodbury opposed an independent treasury as being "less convenient, less secure and more complex, if not more expensive," than the use of state banks.[33]

The administration was taking a middle course between Whig support for a national bank and the Calhounite minority calling for a complete separation of the government from banking. Still, a system of priorities had been established. By apparently endorsing governmental separation from all banks should pet banking collapse, Woodbury was inviting independent treasury advocates to redouble their efforts in Congress.

When James Polk introduced the administration's pet banks regulation bill in Congress in December 1834, Georgia Congressman George Gamble countered with a resolution calling for Treasury opinion as to the feasibility of the government's operating without the use of banks. Polk employed Treasury strategy in arguing that state banks were adequate and a national bank unnecessary; all to no avail. In the previous session the issue had been drawn between Jackson's "executive usurpation" and recharter of the national Bank. Some southern

32. *House Journal*, 23 Cong., 1 sess., 824–829.
33. *Senate Documents*, 23 Cong., 2 sess., no. 13.

Democrats could support neither; now they had an alternative. Gamble informed Polk that his resolution called for an evaluation of governmental separation from all banks, state and national, and praised Jackson's annual message of 1830 in which he had advocated a treasury bank. Augustine Clayton, also of Georgia, challenged the consistency of the administration's position: "If the power of money cannot be trusted in one shape, it is idle to suppose it can in another . . . You may think you have drawn its teeth, by taking the little State banks for your purpose; . . . They will as effectually sting you to death."[34]

The debate embarrassed Polk and other House Democrats, especially since Gamble cited Jackson's own 1830 proposal in support of his resolution. Also, a protracted discussion might have prevented early action on the bill to regulate the deposit banks. Polk forced a vote, which passed 106 to 97, to table the Gamble resolution.[35] Such a close vote indicated that many Whigs realized the nuisance value in supporting the Gamble resolution.

The southern opponents of the state bank system were not finished, however. When Polk opened debate on the bank regulation bill in February 1835, William Gordon countered with a detailed plan for independent treasury operations, which also specified that the government receive and disburse only specie. Whigs then withdrew their support of such a plan and Polk commanded a majority to defeat the Gordon proposal with only a sprinkling of southerners supporting it.[36]

34. *Register of Debates,* 23 Cong., 2 sess., 893–896.
35. *Ibid.,* 902–903.
36. Gordon's speech is an interesting and politically powerful combination of southern sensitivities on the abuses of executive power and sectional jealousy of New York's alleged advantages from Treasury policy. Gordon argued that pet banking operations increased New York banking capital by thirteen millions (*ibid.,* 1281–1288).

But while House Democrats defeated the troublesome Calhounite proposals, explorations into the feasibility of some
sort of independent treasury system were quietly undertaken
within the Treasury department itself. Preliminary proposals
were drafted by Treasury clerk William Gouge, who had
been recommended to Woodbury by the Philadelphia
Quaker-philanthropist Roberts Vaux.[37] "I need not tell thee
how much I dread the Banking system," Vaux wrote Gouge
shortly after the latter's arrival in Washington, encouraging
him to draw up a plan "for keeping and disbursing the public
Treasure, without any connection whatever with any
Banks."[38] Woodbury asked Gouge to put his ideas on paper
and submit them to him in a formal report. By March of 1835
the Gouge proposal was in Woodbury's hands. Gouge
treated the matter in the "abstract," as he explained to the
secretary, since many of the details would depend upon
when the plan was put into effect. It called for subtreasuries
to be located in the customhouses and facilities where the
government currently collected revenue, with separate subtreasuries in a few of the large cities. The plan also proposed
that the government receive and disburse only gold and
silver.[39]

Gouge's preliminary proposal for an independent treasury
was put aside while the administration attempted banking reform through other means. These efforts met with only partial
success. The Bank of the United States' charter would expire
in 1836, and Roberts Vaux and others again urged Gouge to

The Gordon amendment received only thirty-three votes but this is
not an accurate guide to the anti-New York feeling in Congress over
pet banking operations (*ibid.*, 1333–1334).

37. R. Vaux to Woodbury, Dec. 24, 1834, Woodbury Papers.
38. Vaux to Gouge, Jan. 24, 1835, Van Buren Papers.
39. Gouge to Woodbury, April 2, 1835, Woodbury Papers.

submit a formal treatise on an independent treasury to coincide with the Bank's expiration. After receiving encouragement from Kendall, Gouge drafted a more detailed plan which he submitted to Jackson in the summer of 1836, on which Jackson noted "to be carefully perused."[40] Gouge's drafts, reports, publications, and conversations with persons in the administration served as the background for the party's independent treasury bill which Van Buren submitted to the special session of Congress when the Panic of 1837 finally broke the state bank deposit system. Thus the independent treasury proposal was not a measure hastily conceived by Van Buren in political desperation after the financial crisis of 1837; it had been discussed within administration circles for some time. The independent treasury proposal failed to receive widespread Democratic support as long as the use of state banks was feasible, because it represented too great a departure from tradition and involved considerable political risk.

The second session of the Twenty-third Congress was more of a frustrating experience for anti-banking Democrats than the previous session had been. They had been forced to scuttle their own pet banks regulation bill when Whig and anti-Jackson congressmen, in supporting the Binney amendment, posed as even more zealous advocates of bank regulation than the administration stalwarts. The administration's southern opponents had taken a more visible anti-banking stand as well with their disconcerting demands for an independent treasury, a measure they claimed reflected the true hard-money position. By contrast, Democrats were forced to shelter the pets from various attackers and received little in return for their efforts.

40. Gouge to Jackson, Aug. 13, 1836, Jackson Papers.

Before the second session of the Twenty-third Congress ended, Democrats channeled their frustrated energies into a bill calling for the addition of branches to the United States Mint. The Mint was of great symbolic importance to Democrats since it coined bullion into the gold and silver coins synonymous with Jacksonianism. There was some concern, however, that the institution would be unable to produce enough coins to replace bank notes of small denominations. By the winter of 1835 the problem was particularly urgent for Democrats among New York bankers and politicians who had faithfully followed Jacksonian leadership and successfully urged the Democratic legislature to ban all bank notes under $5. Van Buren, Silas Wright and a New York bank commissioner urged Woodbury to speed up Mint operations if the small-note prohibition was to succeed in New York; failure in the Empire State would cast a shadow on Jacksonian reform everywhere, they counseled.[41]

One New Yorker who put great pressure on the Mint and its director, Samuel Moore, was the president of the Bank of America, George Newbold. He was a sincere supporter of small-note restriction and realized its importance to the continuance of sound and stable banking in the country. "The voice of the country will require a reform in the currency," he wrote to Woodbury. "The issue of banks will be wholesomely restricted, the bills of the smaller denomination will be wholly interdicted, and a metallic currency will supply their place." But, as Newbold complained to Woodbury, his bank and the other two deposit banks in New York had planned to send a million dollars in bullion to the Mint for coining, but Moore had advised them that the Mint could

41. Van Buren to Woodbury, Feb. 27, 1835; Wright to Woodbury, Feb. 15, 1835; Charles Stebbins to Wright, Jan. 23, 1835, Letters from Banks.

handle only $200,000 and that it would take ninety days to coin even this amount.[42] Woodbury passed these criticisms along to Moore for an explanation. The Mint director angrily replied that Newbold and other influential New Yorkers actually wanted Mint operations shifted to New York City. Newbold, in turn, wrote to Moore: "It was not that you did not, or could not coin for the *Bank of America*, or for the *City of New York* as we wished, but it was that you did not, nor could not coin for *the country* as the public interests required."[43] In fact, Newbold and other New Yorkers did want a Mint branch in New York City because most of the foreign coins came into their city and it was expensive to send them to Philadelphia for recoining. But Newbold assured Woodbury that the establishment of a Mint branch in New York City could wait; it was more important to augment Philadelphia operations immediately.[44]

A bill authorizing branch mints was introduced in the second session of the Twenty-third Congress. New York City was excluded while branches were proposed for the states of Louisiana, North Carolina, and Georgia. Benton strongly supported the bill in the Senate. Clay led the opposition, arguing that it would increase executive patronage, was too expensive, and was totally unnecessary. Calhoun rejoined the Democrats in support of the measure, claiming that it was of vital importance to the South. (The bill was also important to Calhoun personally because of his financial investments in Georgia gold mines.) The final vote in the Senate broke party lines, with six Democrats joining the Whig opposition. Perhaps interpreting the bill as detrimental to Philadelphia's interests,

42. Newbold to Woodbury, Dec. 9, 1834, *ibid.*
43. Newbold to Woodbury, Jan. 29, 1835; Newbold to Moore, Jan. 27, 1835, *ibid.*
44. Newbold to Woodbury, Dec. 16, 1834, *ibid.*

the two Pennsylvania Democrats voted against it, as did three New England Democrats and one senator from the West. But this group of Democratic dissenters was more than offset by the nine Whigs who joined the Democrats in supporting the bill. These Whigs were all from the South except Webster; the only southern Whig in opposition was John Black of Mississippi. The bill passed through the House by a majority of nearly two to one.[45] Once again Whig support, as in the case of the Coinage Act, prevented Jacksonians from making the legislation a symbolic test of party fidelity to hard money. As the second session of the Twenty-third Congress adjourned in March 1835, Democratic pressures for more independent executive efforts increased, and the Treasury responded with the issuance of the small-note circular previously described. The Treasury would increase its efforts by the end of 1835 to exert other restraining influences on bank credit, as we shall see in the next chapter. But Woodbury's actions only increased congressional pressures in the next session for an end of executive control over public funds. Some political resolution of the controversy over pet bank management clearly was necessary.

The status quo in pet banking had fewer and fewer defenders as the Twenty-fourth Congress convened in December 1835. The administration's pet banks system was all the more vulnerable because of the increasing federal surplus concentrated by Woodbury in a few pet banks. The secretary, acutely aware of this dilemma, anxiously anticipated congressional action. "The *distress* of the country and the Treasury," he wrote to Gideon Welles, "so violently predicted by the Bank panic makers, will be rather to get rid of

45. *Register of Debates*, 23 Cong., 2 sess., 551–552, 576–582, 545–613, 1655–1656.

surplus money than to obtain all wanted for useful purposes."[46]

Woodbury reported to Congress in December 1835 that the administration was opposed to using the public money "for reloaning and for private gain."[47] In the spring of 1836 he replied to the insistent demands of certain bankers that more of the public money be made available for loans, stating that the government "is not in favor of making any Bank whatever the borrowers and lenders of that surplus." He reaffirmed the administration's policy regarding the management of the federal funds since the removal of the deposits: "The present system of Deposit Banks has been adopted merely with a view to fiscal purposes . . . to the safe and convenient keeping of the public money where it is collected and disbursed. Any equalizing of lending out of the public money among the several states has under this system been a mere incident in some cases and not a part of its original design or object in any of them."[48]

Some Democrats, not certain how to deal with the accumulating public surplus in pet banks, began to look upon it as a new "monster." John Niles wrote to Gideon Welles in the spring of 1836: "It would be better . . . that surplus should be thrown in the depth of the ocean, than that it should be the means of leading the government into any unwise and dangerous measures or policy."[49] Faced with an overflowing treasury of paper credits, the average Jacksonian was stunned into inaction and fell back on moralistic pronouncements. "We are all too rich. That is the greatest danger our simple republicans have to contend with," the *Globe* lamented.[50]

46. Woodbury to Welles, Nov. 3, 1835, Welles Papers.
47. *Executive Documents*, 24 Cong., 1 sess., no. 3.
48. Woodbury to Morris Canal and Banking Company, April 16, 1836, Letters to Banks.
49. Niles to Welles, March 3, 1836, Welles Papers.
50. Washington *Globe*, April 29, 1836.

The hope of some Jacksonians that the surplus would some-how vanish was, for a time, translated into official policy. Woodbury had already minimized the size of the surplus in his report to Congress and continued to do so in his private correspondence.[51] Thomas Benton actually believed that no surplus existed. The Missouri senator's hatred of the paper system was so strong he apparently thought he could make the surplus paper credits disappear by mental exertions. "There was no such surplus." It was "all an illusion," he informed his Senate colleagues.[52] Such statements spread confusion throughout party ranks in Congress. "You ask what were the plans of the Administration?" Senator Niles wrote to Gideon Welles after the passage of the Distribution Act. "I answer they had no plans at all—no measure to propose. . . . If they had any plan it seemed to be to deny the existence of the evils and to maintain that there would be no surplus."[53]

Actually the administration did have a proposal for coping with the surplus, namely that it be invested in state stocks.[54] But this plan was thwarted by Democratic disunity in the Senate. In the previous Congress, Calhoun had sponsored legislation dealing with pet banks, but as the Twenty-fourth Congress had a Democratic majority in the Senate, he allowed Silas Wright to take the leadership. More was involved than political protocol; Calhoun preferred that legislation regarding pet banks and the surplus of public money in them originate with the Democrats.[55]

51. Woodbury to J. Garland, March 25, 1836, Woodbury Papers.

52. *Register of Debates*, 24 Cong., 1 sess., 844–845.

53. Niles to Welles, June 25, 1836, Welles Papers.

54. *Register of Debates*, 24 Cong., 1 sess., 1383.

55. Calhoun to James Hammond, June 19, 1836, in J. Franklin Jameson, ed., "Correspondence of John C. Calhoun," *Annual Report of the American Historical Association, 1899* (Washington, 1900) II, 358–360.

The bill which Wright introduced in the Senate to regulate the pet banks was essentially the House bill that Polk had introduced in the last session. He added an amendment, however, originating from Woodbury, that the Treasury surplus exceeding $7 million be invested in state stocks.[56] "Then for the first time, I saw an apparent disturbance among some of our friends," Wright confided to Azariah Flagg later.[57] Calhoun offered an amendment to Wright's bill substituting distribution for the investment in state stocks. The choice before the Senate was between the Calhoun bill of the last session, regulating deposit banks and including the Webster amendment requiring a twenty per cent specie reserve against circulation and deposits, and the Wright bill of the current session, requiring a specie reserve of twenty-five per cent against circulation alone. Added to the latter was the Calhoun amendment calling for distribution of the surplus funds to the states as a substitute for the Wright proposal for investment in state stocks.[58] The "disturbance" that Wright detected among Senate Democrats conceivably may have been confusion over the bewildering set of choices before them.

The disunity within Democratic ranks became apparent in the next few days. A group of Senators led by Nathaniel Tallmadge of New York and William C. Rives of Virginia, soon to become the leaders of the insurgent Conservative Democrats, were out to wrest the party leadership from Benton and others who represented an increasingly anti-bank, anti-credit posture. Their strategy was to lead Wright (and

56. *Register of Debates*, 24 Cong., 1 sess., 1598–1599.
57. Wright to Flagg, Jan. 9, 1837, Flagg Papers. This is a revealing, lengthy letter detailing the maneuvering within Democratic ranks over distribution.
58. See the speeches of Wright and Calhoun on May 27, 1836, explaining the differences between the two bills, *Register of Debates*, 24 Cong., 1 sess., 1598–1603, 1617–1621.

thereby the administration) into supporting a general distribution of the public funds. A Democratic caucus to devise Senate plans regarding banking and distribution proposals was arranged for an evening when Wright was scheduled to have dinner with the president. Wright naively asked Tallmadge to represent his anti-distribution position at the meeting. "I did not then suspect at all that he had been instrumental in getting up the meeting on that evening, and I was content," Wright later confessed.[59] The next morning he was summoned to a meeting at Woodbury's office where he was informed by Benton that Tallmadge, claiming to represent Wright's views at the meeting, had urged support for the Calhoun-sponsored amendment for general distribution of the public funds.[60] Before Wright could repair the damage (debate on the Calhoun and Wright measures began the next day) all the proposals were referred to a select committee with Wright elected as chairman. The nine-member committee, composed of five Democrats and four Whigs, was carefully selected so that two of the Democrats would agree with the four Whigs on a plan for general distribution.[61] The result was that a Democratic committee with Silas Wright, the administration's spokesman, as chairman reported out the Calhoun proposal as the committee's choice.[62]

Wright did not contest the bill strenuously in the Senate. He was sure it would pass but he hoped to divide the distribu-

59. Wright to Flagg, Jan. 9, 1837, Flagg Papers.

60. *Ibid.*

61. *Senate Journal*, 24 Cong., 1 sess., 394. The two committee Democrats who voted with the four Whigs were Shepley and Hendricks (Wright to Flagg, Jan. 9, 1837, Flagg Papers).

62. *Senate Journal*, 24 Cong., 1 sess., 403. Wright informed his Senate colleagues that the bill was not unanimously agreed to in committee as reported in the press (*Register of Debates*, 24 Cong., 1 sess., 1693).

tion measure from those sections of the bill regulating the pet banks.[63] He did repeat the arguments that had been used in the House debate against the provision calling for a twenty per cent specie reserve against a bank's circulation and deposits, pointing out that such a reserve ratio would make it impossible for western and southwestern banks to operate but would work no hardship on the eastern banks. Rather than endanger the bill's passage, Calhoun moved to strike out his own provision on the grounds that it would operate unjustly against the southwestern banks.[64] The specie reserve clause was deleted in favor of one giving the Secretary of the Treasury discretionary power to require banks to hold a certain amount of specie.

Efforts to divide bank regulation from the distribution feature of the bill were narrowly defeated. The administration would be forced to accept distribution in order to get the bank regulation it had repeatedly sought. Wright had anticipated the passage of the Deposit-Distribution Act but he was surprised by the overwhelming vote, as only six Democrats opposed it.[65] The Calhoun strategy had been successful: the bill was a Democratic measure from beginning to end.

63. Wright to Flagg, Jan. 9, 1837, Flagg Papers.

64. Calhoun vigorously attacked Wright's bill in Senate debate because its specie reserve section did not cover deposits, but when his own bill was endangered, Calhoun moved to strike out the specie clause (*Register of Debates,* 24 Cong., 1 sess., 1620–1621, 1763). It was Wright who then proposed that the secretary be given discretionary power to impose specie reserves upon deposit bank liabilities (*ibid.,* 1764). Webster also insisted upon specie reserve ratios to cover deposits as amendments to the administration's bank regulations bill but lost his enthusiasm for the clause when it was attached to distribution. The Massachusetts Senator thought such a restriction might protect "the general circulation against violent shocks. But I do not attach great importance to this" (*ibid.,* 1650–1651).

65. *Senate Journal,* 24 Cong., 1 sess., 434, 437, 441, 447–448.

The Conservative leadership made every effort to take credit for the measure, heralding it as their alternative to Benton's extremist hard-money views. On the day of final passage, both Rives and Tallmadge made gratuitous speeches in support of the bill.[66] Fellow Democrat John Niles felt both Senators "went much further than was necessary" in declaring their approval of the measure.[67] Tallmadge portrayed distribution as a defense of the credit system, "the invention of modern time" as he called it, and warned the Senate against those who would curtail economic growth with their visionary schemes of hard money.[68] There had been considerable comment on the apparent jealousy between Rives and Benton over party leadership. "The schism may not be permanent, but I am inclined to think it lies pretty deep, and will not be easy to heal," was Calhoun's analysis of the intraparty feud after the speeches.[69]

The vote on distribution, however, does not indicate that the Democratic party was moving in the direction that Tallmadge would have wished, but rather that Democrats as a party found the status quo in pet banking politically untenable, and the Conservative leadership simply championed the most politically expedient alternative. Without strong and effective administration guidance to oppose distribution, Democrats followed Conservative leadership. John Niles called the distribution proposal in February of 1836 "the most alarming bill ever before Congress." Four months later he voted for it, explaining to Gideon Welles, "I thought it best

66. *Register of Debates*, 24 Cong., 1 sess., 1821–1837.
67. Niles to Welles, June 18, 1836, Welles Papers.
68. *Register of Debates*, 24 Cong., 1 sess., 1826–1830.
69. Calhoun to James Hammond, June 19, 1836, "Correspondence of Calhoun," 358–361.

to vote for it when I found that most of our friends were going that way."[70]

Most Democrats were "going that way," as Niles put it, because they felt they had no alternative. To oppose a distribution of the public money would certainly have opened a wider breach between the Conservative and administration Democrats. Silas Wright, Van Buren's spokesman in the Senate, received no encouragement from Van Buren to wage a campaign against the measure; to do so might have reduced his chances at the polls in November. Still, Van Buren was opposed to distribution and said so, which made it hard to charge him with inconsistency.

The most formidable argument against Democratic opposition to a distribution of the public money was that such opposition would have put the party on the side of the pet banks and against returning the public money to the people. "The pockets of the people, are the safest depository of their own money," a Democratic congressmen stated to Governor David Campbell of Virginia.[71] This was not a very sophisticated economic argument, but it was difficult to quarrel with its political appeal. "I believe it to be essential to our interests as a party," Richard Parker wrote to Van Buren, "to make some disposition of the surplus, other than suffering it to remain in the selected Banks."[72] The same argument was used repeatedly and effectively during the Senate debate. James Buchanan of Pennsylvania advised fellow Democrats that it was a choice between distributing the money to the states or leaving it in the pet banks. He reminded his colleagues that the opposition accused them of using the money in the pets to

70. Niles to Welles, Feb. 25, June 18, 1836, Welles Papers.
71. G. Hopkins to Campbell, June 23, 1836, Campbell Papers.
72. Parker to Van Buren, June 29, 1836, Van Buren Papers.

help friends and influence elections. While he thought such a charge nonsense, he had to admit it was good politics and the only way to discredit it was to deposit the money with the states.[73] Tallmadge, while claiming to have the utmost confidence in the pets, argued that they were unable to use all the funds. He pointed out the discrepancy in the position of those who claimed to distrust all banks but were willing to leave the public funds in them rather than deposit the money with the states.[74] John Niles perceptively recorded the dilemma in which the Democrats found themselves when writing to Gideon Welles that the effect of a veto of the distribution bill by Jackson "would be to continue perhaps for two years, 20 or 30 millions in the Deposite Banks—the veto would be said to be against the states and *for* the Banks, instead of *against* the Banks, as in 1832."[75] Again the Jacksonian rhetoric had backfired on the administration, and this time prevented it from pursuing currency reform through a selected few state banks.

One significant victory for Jacksonian anti-bank forces during the first session of the Twenty-fourth Congress concerned the expansion of Mint operations. By May of 1835 the energetic Robert M. Patterson had replaced Samuel Moore as Mint director. Patterson promised the administration increased efficiency in coinage of the precious metals and quickly substituted steam driven machines for manual ones.[76] It was his suggestion that Mint financial operations be significantly altered. The Mint at that time was coining only the bullion

73. *Register of Debates*, 24 Cong., 1 sess., 1803–1804.
74. An obvious reference to Benton, *ibid.*, 1837.
75. Niles to Welles, June 21, 1836, Welles Papers.
76. R. M. Patterson to Jackson, May 29, 1835, Jackson Papers; Patterson to Woodbury, Nov. 13, 1835, United States Treasury Department Records, Letters from Mint, National Archives.

brought to it and was therefore a passive agent in introducing gold and silver into circulation. Patterson urged that the Mint be made a special depository of the federal government, thus making it possible to coin bullion in advance.

The new director explained the sporadic nature of Mint operations to Woodbury while pointing out the necessary remedy: "Deposits do not flow in upon us regularly, but we are sometimes left almost idle, and sometimes, as at the present moment, overwhelmed with bullion. Now if we had a deposite from the government . . . this might be coined at our more leisure times, and could be paid from time to time to individual depositors, their bullion taking its place."[77] Patterson made this the main point of his report to Congress for the year 1835. In forwarding the report Jackson heartily endorsed the plan.[78] Benton, already aware of the Mint's difficulty, agreed with Patterson's suggestions. He wrote Woodbury in January 1836, shortly after Congress convened: "We must make the Mints depositories, in common with the Banks, for public monies, whereby they will always be supplied with bullion and foreign coins."[79] A few days later, Benton submitted a resolution asking the Secretary of the Treasury to inform the Senate whether or not the Mint was regularly supplied with bullion, and inviting him to suggest alternatives to present Mint operations. As Benton knew it would, Woodbury's reply stated that bullion sent to the Mint was "quite inadequate" and suggested legislation authorizing him to transfer specie from the deposit banks to the Mint in order to keep it steadily employed in coining bullion.[80]

Benton and other Senate Democrats succeeded in giving the

77. R. M. Patterson to Woodbury, Nov. 19, 1835, *ibid.*
78. *Executive Documents*, 24 Cong., 1 sess., no. 76.
79. Benton to Woodbury, Jan. 6, 1836, Woodbury Papers.
80. *Senate Journal*, 24 Cong., 1 sess., 149.

secretary such authorization through an amendment to the Deposit-Distribution Act of 1836. The administration officially supported the measure, and its incorporation into the Distribution Act undoubtedly softened Jackson's opposition to the bill. Blair's explanation of the new use of the Mint clearly indicates that its function was not only to augment gold coinage but to supply a necessary check on the note issues of banks as well. "Drafts could be given from time to time on the deposite banks for the necessary supplies," he informed readers of the *Globe*, "say $50,000, 100,000 or 500,000 at a time . . . Thus, the paper issues of the deposite banks would be held in check, and thus the dangers of a paper revenue would be diminished."[81] Benton regarded depository status for the Mint as a welcome alternative to governmental reliance upon state banks. As he stated during Senate debate on the proposal: "Let the banks see that the United States are not dependent upon them for keeping the public monies and are in a condition to dictate terms, or to cut the connection with all banking establishments."[82]

The influence of the legislation was never tested. It was already too late to offset the 1836 inflation which contributed to the economy's collapse in the spring of 1837. Yet despite its shortcomings, the example of the Mint proposal is further evidence that influential Democrats sought to restrain the financial boom which they had unwittingly stimulated.

The congressional action, or lack of it, during these years points to the divergent forces within the Jacksonian political movement as it struggled to develop national policies on banking. Some Democrats urged that Jacksonianism stand for unflinching hostility toward banking in general. This group very early called for a clean separation of the government

81. Washington *Globe,* Feb. 4, 1836.
82. *Register of Debates,* 24 Cong., 1 sess., 1092.

from banking in order to preserve a Jacksonianism untainted by any association with the "money power." A second group of Democrats, emerging as Conservatives in the struggle over the Specie Circular, argued for a financial nexus between the federal government and state banks. These Democrats saw in such a partnership a future without the danger of a national bank but with the advantages of a mild currency reform to satisfy the hard-money zealots within the party. Trying to steer a middle course between these two positions was a third group, the Democratic advocates of banking regulation. Sometimes confused over what to regulate and how, they were in the uneviable position of urging a closer association between the government and pet banks in order to make banking more responsible. The advocates of regulation operated best *sub rosa*, or when their purposes were concealed under the rubric of hard money, but it was difficult to deny the fact that the government's pet banking policy meant preferential treatment for certain banks.

Congressional debate on the issues of an independent treasury, hard money, and expanded Mint operations provides insight into the political and economic difficulties of the Democratic position on banking. The anti-banking posture of the party was most forcefully represented by the Gouge proposal for an independent treasury. This concept embodied a negative approach to federal responsibility for banks and credit, since the banking community would be left to regulate itself after the government withdrew its resources and potential controls. The federal government, by receiving and disbursing specie, would only indirectly influence bank credit. The independent treasury's great advantage lay in dissolving the association between government and banking, thus restoring the moral and political integrity of governmental action.

The proposal to use the Mint as a federal depository reveals more about the complicated moods of Democrats toward banks and credit. Expanded governmental use of the Mint promised increased coinage of gold and silver, as well as providing a depository for government funds. These features of the Mint proposal attracted the anti-banking, hard-money advocates typified by Senator Benton. But the projected use of the Mint also included flexible regulations on bank credit and for that reason attracted those Democrats more reconciled than Benton to bank-generated paper credit. The Mint, therefore, became the magic institution in which Democratic advocates of banking regulations were reconciled with the less sophisticated opponents of all banks, the two groups having found common ground in hard money.

6

The Domesticated Pets: Treasury Regulation

The divisive Jacksonian rhetoric and unpredictability of congressional action made Levi Woodbury's task as Secretary of the Treasury difficult, if not impossible. Basically, Woodbury needed to develop a Treasury policy that could gain the confidence of the banking community and still retain the support of powerful anti-banking Democrats. But these particular Democrats considered a satisfied banking community evidence of financial conspiracy, and evaluated Treasury proposals on the basis of the amount of opposition they generated within financial circles.

Woodbury's management of pet banking operations depended upon cooperation between the Washington Treasury and Wall Street bankers. This relationship was necessary from an economic point of view: New York City was the financial capital of America, her port handled a large volume of American imports and exports, and international monetary exchange operations were centered in Wall Street.

New York's financial advantages were complemented by alleged extensive political influence upon Washington policy. The New York Democracy, astutely led by the strategically situated Van Buren, supposedly insured maximum benefits to the Empire State from Treasury policy. The ostensible Treasury favoritism of the Wall Street "money power" acutely embarrassed zealous anti-bank Democrats and seemed to validate the charge that the Bank War was a Regency-inspired plan for profits and political power. But Treasury policy made it necessary to favor some banks, and Woodbury's decision to concentrate funds on Wall Street was fiscally sound, if politically troublesome.

New York Regency Democrats were, in fact, progressively dissatisfied with Treasury policy. Basic to this dissatisfaction was the division within the New York banking community between city and country banks. Regency interests were scattered among the upstate country banks with headquarters in the Albany Mechanics and Farmers Bank. Van Buren did attempt to establish some Regency influence over the state's pet banking operations by suggesting that Thomas Olcott, cashier of the Mechanics and Farmers Bank, be consulted on the selection of New York pets.[1] Though the New York deposit banks selected were in Democratic or politically neutral hands,[2] there is no evidence that Olcott had anything to do with Treasury selections. More important to an understanding of pet banking and the New York Democracy is the fact that all three New York deposit banks—the Bank of America, The Manhattan Company and the Mechanics Bank —were located in New York City.

New York Democrats pressured Woodbury for an expansion of pet banking operations in New York in order to disperse Treasury benefits among the rural banking interests. Regency Democrats saw little hope that Woodbury could

1. Van Buren to Jackson, Sept. 4, 1833, *Correspondence of Andrew Jackson*, V, 181–182.
2. Frank Otto Gatell, "Spoils of the Bank War," *American Historical Review*, LXX (1964), 43–47.

select rural banks while the more substantial city banks had greater claims, but at the least they wanted Treasury appointment of city banks that had important financial relationships with favored upstate banks. The New York City Phoenix bank falling into this category, it was recommended to Woodbury by New York Governor William Marcy, Senator Nathaniel Tallmadge, as well as John Dix and Greene Bronson.[3] Regency interest in the Phoenix bank (aside from alleged heavy stockholdings)[4] resulted from the correspondent relationship between it and the Albany City Bank, the latter being a particular Regency favorite along with the Albany Mechanics and Farmers.[5]

In a letter to George Newbold in December 1835, Watts Sherman, the Albany City Bank cashier, explained the important relationship between the Albany bank and the New York City Phoenix bank. "We concentrate the collection of about twenty Banks in the interior of this State, Ohio, and Michigan," and all of these notes payable in New York, "pass into the hands of our corresponding Bank in that City," Sherman explained to Newbold. He was proposing a shift of the Albany City Bank's account from the Phoenix to the Bank of America, presumably because the Regency had failed to persuade Woodbury to select the Phoenix. "We would prefer being

3. Marcy to Jackson, March 19, 1835; Tallmadge to Jackson, March 19, 1835; John Dix to Woodbury, May 12, 1835; Greene Bronson to Woodbury, May 14, 1835, Letters from Banks.

4. New York *Evening Post*, June 3, 1834.

5. After the passage of the Distribution Act, the Albany City Bank was recommended to the Treasury by imposing Regency figures such as Van Buren, Silas Wright, John Dix, Azariah Flagg and Governor Marcy (Van Buren to Woodbury, Sept. 21, 1836; Silas Wright to Woodbury, June 9, 1936; Dix, Flagg, and Marcy to Woodbury, July 8, 1836, United States Treasury Department Records, Recommendations of Banks, National Archives).

with one of the deposit Banks," Sherman confided. The corresponding relationship would be financially reciprocal since Sherman expected Newbold's Bank of America to "give to us your entire collection in this City, the interior of the State, etc."[6]

A more successful Regency attempt to derive benefits from Washington Treasury policy involved the Mechanics and Farmers bank. The Treasury had carried a nominal deposit with this Albany Regency bank of twenty-five dollars throughout 1833 and 1834, but in 1835 it was appointed a full time pet, and the government balance swelled to over $100,000 by the end of the year. At the same time, however, $5.5 million in federal funds were on deposit in the three Wall Street pets. Thomas Olcott, cashier of the Mechanics and Farmers Bank, was impatient with Treasury preference for Wall Street banks and urged Woodbury to shift still more of the deposits to his upstate bank. The secretary curtly replied that "the Department as a general principle makes no transfers of public moneys to Banks, which do not collect it unless to places where it is wanted for disbursement or for safety."[7] This "general principle" meant that without a dramatic expansion of Treasury operations or the appointment of correspondent city banks such as the Phoenix, Democratic country banks would not benefit directly from pet banking policy.

6. Watts Sherman to George Newbold, Dec. 7, 1835, Newbold Papers, New York Public Library.

7. *Executive Documents*, 24 Cong., 2 sess., no. 77; Woodbury to Olcott, Nov. 5, 1835, Letters to Banks. Woodbury advised his three Wall Street pets to follow a "course of comity and indulgence . . . towards any new Banking Institutions in their neighbourhood" (Woodbury to Bank of America, Mechanics Bank, and The Manhattan Company, Jan. 30, 1835, Letters to Banks). Needless to say, the "neighbourhood" of Wall Street did not extend to Albany.

The New York Democracy's quarrel with Treasury policy was carried to the pages of the Regency press, the Albany *Argus*. Secretary Woodbury's annual report for 1835 advised against pet banking expansion, stating that additional Treasury selections were unnecessary and would only endanger the public funds. The Albany *Argus* courteously but firmly replied to Woodbury's statement. "As a general proposition this may be sound," the Regency press declared. "But it is open to exceptions, and particularly in relation to the existing deposit banks in this state."[8] Regency Democrats would be only too happy to provide the secretary with the "exceptions" they had in mind. But the Washington *Globe,* responding to the *Argus'* editorial, made it clear that the administration supported Woodbury's nonexpansionist Treasury policy.[9]

Regency Democrats continued to press Woodbury for additional pet bank selections, as did many others, but they were frustrated in their efforts until the passage of the Distribution Act in July 1836 forced additional bank selections in New York as well as elsewhere. Eager recommendations poured into the Treasury from Regency circles promoting the services of the solidly Democratic country banks.[10] The pro-

8. Albany *Argus,* Dec. 16, 1835.
9. Washington *Globe,* Jan. 7, 1836.
10. Aside from the Albany City Bank and Phoenix Bank already mentioned, Regency Democrats recommended, among others, the Bank of Troy and the Canal Bank of Albany (Marcy, Dix, and Flagg to Woodbury, July 13, 1836, Letters from Banks, for the Bank of Troy). See also Woodbury's letter to Tallmadge, explaining his refusal to appoint the Troy Bank (July 18, 1836, Letters to Banks). Recommendations for the Canal Bank came from Dix, Flagg, and Silas Wright. See their letters to Woodbury for July 13, 1836 (Recommendations of Banks). It is important to note that the Canal Bank held $22,325 in stock of the New York City Greenwich Bank (New York *Assembly Documents,* 1833, no. 89). Both Marcy and C. C. Cambreleng urged Woodbury to appoint the Greenwich Bank

cedure forced upon the Treasury by distribution was a very different policy from that previously implemented by Woodbury. Had the business community been less dissatisfied with Treasury policy, distribution would have been unnecessary; the new law was the result of financial and political resentment against Woodbury's management of the public funds which was, in the opinion of his critics, too regulatory, too deflationary, and too selective.

Woodbury's refusal to appoint additional pet banks in New York before 1836 not only left upstate Regency Democrats unsatisfied, the economic impact of this policy affected the entire state of New York directly, and the nation indirectly. New York pet banks not only were subject to Treasury direction but were regulated by the state's Safety Fund Act in addition.[11] This law limited the loans of any New York bank to two and one-half times that of its capital.[12] Such a restriction meant that regardless of the amount of public money Woodbury concentrated on Wall Street, bank loans based on these funds were limited to the ratio imposed by the Safety Fund Act. Expansionist critics of Woodbury's policy, therefore, charged that the public money lay idle in Wall Street banks. Demands for a more flexible money market were directed at the government, because government receipts, a quick source of credit, accumulated rapidly in pet banks after the national debt retirement in 1834.

---

as a pet after the Distribution Act (Marcy to Woodbury, Aug. 31, 1836; Cambreleng to Woodbury, Sept. 5, 1836, Recommendations of Banks).

11. The Manhattan Company was not affected by Safety Fund restrictions but adjusted its financial activities to correspond to the act's regulations (John J. Palmer to Woodbury, May 14, 1835 [copy], Jackson Papers).

12. Chaddock, *The Safety Fund,* 262–263.

Critiques of Jacksonian economic policy should begin with a clear understanding of the administration's attitude and actions affecting the public funds in pet banks between 1834 and 1836. Harry N. Scheiber has challenged the traditional laissez-faire theory of Jacksonian finance. He finds that pet banks as a group maintained a one-third specie reserve against circulation during those years and that Woodbury urged pet banks to hold a one-fourth specie reserve against circulation after the passage of the inflationary Distribution-Deposit Act of the summer of 1836. The crucial consideration, however, in the relationship between pet banking policy and inflation, as Scheiber points out, was the rapid accumulation of public deposits in pet banks throughout 1836. When these deposits were taken into account (along with note circulation, private deposits, and sums due to banks), the ratio of specie to demand liabilities of pet banks decreased sharply; in this way, pet banking practices dangerously expanded bank credit. "Unfortunately," Scheiber continues, "Woodbury imposed no regulations governing specie reserves for deposit-bank liabilities other than circulation." It was not Woodbury's intentions which were at fault, according to Scheiber, but his lack of economic sophistication and consequent failure to impose realistic restraints upon the government's pet banks.[13]

However, a closer look at Treasury policy concerning pet banking reveals that Woodbury did recognize the crucial relationship of specie to total demand liabilities and took steps to improve that ratio among the leading pet banks, particularly the three Wall Street pets. As previously stated, the critical factor in determining a bank's soundness or liquidity is the ratio between its immediate assets (specie) and its total de-

13. Harry N. Scheiber, "The Pet Banks in Jacksonian Politics and Finance, 1833–1841," *Journal of Economic History*, XXIII (1963), 196–214.

mand liabilities (notes in circulation, public and private deposits, and sums due to banks). Using this guide, the three Wall Street pets followed relatively sound financial practices throughout most of 1835. Taken as a group, these banks had a liquidity ratio in February 1835 of 22 per cent. (Some members of Congress during a debate over the Distribution-Deposit Act recommended a ratio of 20 per cent as a safe guideline for government banks to follow.) By November 1835, government deposits in the three Wall Street pets had tripled, raising the banks' liabilities markedly and thus affecting their liquidity ratio. The ratio fell from 22 per cent to 15 per cent by November 1835. It did not fall further because these three banks reduced their private deposits (from $4.7 million to $3.5) as well as funds due to banks (from $3.9 to $2.2 million).[14] Since deposit creation was replacing note issue as a means of extending credit by the larger commercial banks, the decrease in private deposits while government funds were increasing adds substance to the argument that pet banking policy was adding to, rather than relieving, the pressure in the money market.

Increasing federal deposits in the Wall Street pets by fall of 1835 forced Woodbury to take additional steps to regulate bank credit expansion. In October 1835, the secretary ordered the three New York pet banks to increase specie holdings to one-half the amount of their public deposits.[15] In order to assess the financial impact of Woodbury's specie order, the condition of the Wall Street pets near the end of 1835 should be analyzed. In November these banks held approximately $8.5 million of public funds (approximately one-third of the total) and $2.5 million in specie. To carry out Woodbury's

14. *Senate Documents*, 24 Cong., 1 sess., no. 2.
15. Woodbury to Bank of America, Mechanics Bank, and The Manhattan Company, Oct. 5, 1835, Letters to Banks.

order required them to increase their specie holdings by $2 million collectively. That it was within their financial means to do so is clear since they held over $3 million in notes of other banks.[16]

Woodbury ordered other pet banks to increase specie also. In issuing such directives, the secretary was motivated by more than an unsophisticated commitment to bullionism, as indicated in a letter written in October 1835 to the two Boston pets, the Commonwealth Bank and the Merchants Bank. Woodbury called the bankers' attention "to the small amount of specie in your vaults compared with the public and individual deposites, your circulation and balances due to other banks, for the purpose of suggesting to you the propriety of increasing the amount to meet any unforeseen emergencies."[17] The Secretary of the Treasury was attempting to impose a specie reserve policy upon the leading pets to create greater liquidity; he continued to do so throughout 1836.[18]

Woodbury maintained his specie reserve policy toward selected pet banks, held the line on the number of banks, and

16. *Senate Documents*, 24 Cong., 1 sess., no. 2.

17. Woodbury to Commonwealth Bank and The Merchants Bank, Oct. 9, 1835, Letters to Banks.

18. Woodbury did emphasize specie reserves against circulation, but it is also true that most banks, especially those in the interior, relied heavily upon note issue as a means of credit expansion. Woodbury was not overlooking the role of deposits in bank liabilities, only recognizing the different practices of interior banks from the more commercial banks along the eastern seaboard. For example, Woodbury cautioned the Branch Bank of Alabama at Mobile about its low stock of specie compared to its "circulation and other immediate liabilities" (Woodbury to Branch Bank of Alabama at Mobile, May 18, 1836, Letters to Banks). In his annual report for 1835, Woodbury reported that specie in a number of pet banks had been "increased in comparison with their issues and deposits" (*Executive Documents*, 24 Cong., 1 sess., no. 3).

concentrated the public money along the eastern seaboard, despite growing criticism of this course of action. The secretary planned to use his annual report to Congress in December 1835 to defend pet banking operations. He labored through November to gather as much information as possible, especially with respect to the charge that an increasing amount of the public money was lying idle in Wall Street vaults. That same month, the request by the Morris Canal and Banking Company to be appointed a deposit bank afforded Woodbury the occasion to elaborate upon his policy.

The Morris Canal and Banking Company operated under a New Jersey charter, but New York City financial interests dominated the company and its operations were mainly in that city. The bank argued that its appointment as a pet bank would ease the money market in New York City since its financial operations under a New Jersey charter were not subject to the restrictions of the New York Safety Fund Act. Woodbury asked his Wall Street bankers to reply to the complaint that Treasury policy and Safety Fund Act restrictions resulted in an unusually restrictive money market. The Wall Street bankers promptly and vigorously defended Treasury policy and questioned the wisdom of making any changes.[19] Naturally the self-interest of the Wall Street pets might dictate their support of the status quo in pet banking, but this immediate consideration was coupled with Wall Street's concern for a regulated and safe banking system, as their answers to Woodbury show. Robert White, cashier of

19. H. Jerome Cramer, "Improvements without Public Funds: The New Jersey Canals," 115–166, in Carter Goodrich, ed., *Government Promotion of American Canals and Railroads, 1800–1840* (New York 1961), 141–146; Daniel Jackson and John S. Crary to Woodbury, Nov. 21, 1835, Newbold Papers (copy); Robert White to Woodbury, Nov. 17, 1835, George Newbold to Woodbury, Nov. 17, 1835, Letters from Banks.

the Manhattan Company, pointed out that he had seen Woodbury's October order to increase specie as necessitating the reduction of loans by the Wall Street pets. To appoint additional banks in New York City, he continued, "would seem to lessen the conservative power of the Treasury department over the currency . . . which enables it to secure to the people of the United States an enlarging basis of gold and silver in that currency."[20] John Fleming, Mechanics Bank president, advised Woodbury that in place of ordinary bank loans, the New York pets allowed balances to stand with other city banks, thus enabling the pets to improve their creditor position.[21] The influential George Newbold declared that not all the public money could be used in loans, pointing out that enough credit was already outstanding, either directly or "through the credit and indulgence" of the pets to other city banks.[22] Campbell P. White, former New York City congressman and brother of Robert White, admitted that a growing demand for credit existed but defended Treasury policy on the grounds that "it has a manifest tendency to check overtrading in banks and individuals and to repress the spirit of gambling and speculation which is now almost universal." He praised Woodbury's specie order as "a measure of that conservative character that cannot fail to have the best effects."[23]

A few days later Woodbury pressed the Wall Street bankers for a more detailed defense against the charge that they were not usefully employing the public money. The same day, November 21, he had received a long letter from Daniel Jackson and John S. Crary, two Morris Canal board mem-

20. White to Woodbury, Nov. 17, 1835, Letters from Banks.
21. Fleming to Woodbury, Nov. 17, 1835, Letters from Banks.
22. Newbold to Woodbury, Nov. 17, 1835, Letters from Banks.
23. C. P. White to Woodbury, Nov. 20, 1835, Woodbury Papers.

bers, who spelled out their specific complaints against the practices of the New York City pets.[24] Woodbury passed along these criticisms, not because he thought they were valid but because he wanted the detailed replies of the Wall Street bankers as support for his annual report to Congress the next month. In acknowledging their letters, Woodbury replied to Jackson and Crary: "Some views suggested by you as to the present Deposit Banks in New York and which do not correspond with the impressions of this Department will . . . in a few days be answered."[25]

On November 23, two days after receiving the directors' letter and before receiving the expected defensive replies of the Wall Street bankers, Woodbury answered the charges of the Morris Canal and Banking Company. His letter to them represents one of Woodbury's longest statements of Treasury policy and, along with his annual report to Congress the next month, the fullest explanation of Jacksonian pet banking operations. The specific complaint of the representatives of the Morris Canal and Banking Company had been that the New York pets could not use enough of the public money in loans. "The pressing demands of the public for increased money facilities" could not be satisfied in New York because of the restrictions of the Safety Fund Act, Jackson and Crary explained, but their company, under a New Jersey charter, could "discount *ad libitum*."[26] Woodbury, in his reply, touched upon the administration's sensitivity about the in-

24. Woodbury to Bank of America, Mechanics Bank, and The Manhattan Company, Nov. 21, 1835, Letters to Banks; Jackson and Crary to Woodbury, Nov. 21, 1835, Newbold Papers (copy).

25. Woodbury to Jackson and Crary, Nov. 21, 1835, Letters to Banks.

26. Jackson and Crary to Woodbury, Nov. 21, 1835, Newbold Papers.

creasing amount of public money on deposit in Wall Street banks, terming the $7 million presently on deposit there an "excessive proportion," much of which resulted from public land sales. The Morris Canal and Banking Company had asked only to share funds not already on deposit, but Woodbury explained that additional money in New York would only be there for a short time prior to expenditure or "such disposition as it is expected Congress at an early day will direct." Until Congress took action on this "delicate subject," Woodbury reported, it was "the settled policy of the President and the Department to make as few changes as possible . . . in the present number and system of the Deposit Banks."

Furthermore, the secretary disputed the contention that all the public money in New York "ought to be employed in ordinary bank loans." Woodbury insisted that the security of the public money was of primary importance. The pet banks, therefore, were required to pledge security for the funds they held whenever the amount exceeded one-half the bank's capital. In addition, Woodbury pointed out that while Congress had not yet passed legislation regulating pet banks, it had sanctioned the principle of a specie reserve for deposit banks equal to one-fourth or one-fifth of their immediate liabilities. Another objective of Treasury policy was the gradual replacement of small-denomination bank notes with specie. For these reasons, Woodbury explained, he had instructed the New York City pets to increase their holdings of specie, an action which he anticipated would reduce the amount of public money available for loans to about $3.5 million. Concerning the use of this money for business purposes, he lauded the practice of the New York City pets of employing it "in the form of balances allowed to stand against other banks and of large amounts of notes against other banks not presented for payment, rather than use the whole in private and individual loans and obtain on it interest."[27]

The strongest and fullest defense of New York City pet banking policy came from George Newbold of the Bank of America. His concern for a carefully regulated, conservative banking system was of long standing, and his respected position on Wall Street accounted for his influence on Treasury policy. Daniel Jackson of the Morris Canal and Banking Company had supplied Newbold with a copy of his letter to the Treasury recognizing his and the Bank of America's importance to Treasury operations. Accordingly, Newbold was able to answer the charges contained in the letter in some detail. Advising a general restraint on banking operations, he stated, "In times of general prosperity like the present, there is danger that both banks and the commercial community will go too far." To increase loans temporarily would satisfy the existing demand for credit but would only put off the day when a more severe contraction would be necessary. Increased pet bank loans would encourage expanded bank credit everywhere: "The specie funds of all would be thereby lessened when they ought to be enlarged." Newbold significantly shifted his emphasis in refuting the charge that the Wall Street pets lent no more in proportion to their capitals than did other banks in the state, despite the public money they held. His answer was that "the other local Banks have been enabled greatly to extend their loans thru the indulgence extended to them by the Deposit Banks." Should the public money on deposit in Wall Street pets increase, he assured Woodbury, "the same liberal policy which has regulated the course of the Bank of America would enable the community to enjoy the just benefit of the accumulation thru the en-

27. Woodbury to Jackson and Crary, Nov. 23, 1835, Letters to Banks.

larged indulgence that would be extended to the other local banks."[28]

These comments might be interpreted as a tongue-in-cheek use of Jacksonian rhetoric by the wily banker while he reaped the rewards of pet banking. However, the condition of the Bank of America indicates that financially Newbold practiced what he preached. In February 1835, a little over a year after the advent of the pet banks system, the liquidity ratio (specie to private and public deposits, notes in circulation, and sums due to banks) of the Bank of America was a conservative 36 per cent. By November 1835, government deposits were up sharply (from $1.2 million to $3.2 million) and the liquidity ratio of Newbold's bank fell to 17 per cent. By the following February, in accordance with Woodbury's specie order, Newbold increased his holding of specie from $900,000 to approximately $1.3 million and the liquidity ratio of his bank went up to 21 per cent. During this same period (February 1835 to February 1836), the loans and discounts of the Bank of America only increased from $3.6 million to $4.4 million, still a half-million below the maximum allowed by the Safety Fund Act and far too low in the opinion of the bank's many critics, considering the increase in public deposits.[29] The alleged financial plum of being chosen a pet bank had not significantly altered Newbold's commitment to conservative banking principles, as is evident from the liquidity ratio of his bank during a period preceding removal. An analysis of the financial condition of the Bank of America on January 1, 1828, shows a liquidity ratio of 25 per cent.[30] Newbold's

28. Newbold to Woodbury, Nov. 30, 1835, Letters from Banks; Newbold to Woodbury, Dec. 1835, Newbold Papers.

29. *Senate Documents*, 24 Cong., 1 sess., nos. 2 and 226.

30. The Bank of America financial statement was sent to me by Professor J. Van Fenstermaker, Department of Economics, Kent State University.

efforts to maintain a similar ratio after his bank became a pet were even more conservative, since the largest single liability —the federal deposits—was not as likely to be suddenly withdrawn as other demand liabilities.

Newbold's banking practices do not fit the stereotype of nineteenth century wildcat banking operations. A kind of bank credit expansion had taken place, however, which was based upon federal funds, one which played an influential role on the further development of the administration's fiscal policies. As indicated in the letters of Newbold and others, a sub-pet bank system had emerged under which the original pets left balances in other banks of their own choosing—a significant innovation in Wall Street pet bank operations. The total of these balances increased from $1.9 million in February 1835 to $4.2 million one year later.[31] This type of credit expansion placed the original pets in a position somewhat similar to the former BUS branches. Upon orders from the Treasury, the New York City pets could press their debtor banks for specie, forcing them to curtail loans. During financial pressure, and under no contrary Treasury orders, the creditor banks could allow balances to stand and accumulate bank notes until circumstances dictated otherwise. The administration was consciously encouraging such a course of action and, in doing so, emulating one of the much lauded BUS functions. A Woodbury memorandum of July 1836 explicitly stated that Treasury policy was analogous to former BUS operations in that deposit banks were creditors of other state banks and could thereby return their notes for specie whenever note issue became excessive.[32] The Jacksonians were working toward a more decentralized banking operation,

31. *Senate Documents*, 24 Cong., 1 sess., nos. 1 and 226.
32. Woodbury memorandum (July 1836), Van Buren Papers.

more in line with their Jeffersonian prejudices against federal power and their affinity for states rights.

By December 1835, the administration had made it clear that the "experiment" of pet banking was an established system, still in need of legislative regulation and more extensive prohibition of small-denomination bank notes, but requiring few changes in the general principles under which the public money was being managed. Woodbury's December Treasury report to Congress made public the opinions he had formulated in his exchanges with the Morris Canal and Banking Company and the New York City pets. He assured his many critics that the public money would continued to be used as an aid to business. But for "reasons of public importance," Woodbury explained, he had ordered "that the specie in the vaults of a number of the selected Banks, should be still more increased in comparison with their issues and deposits." The continuing program of substituting gold and silver for bank notes of small denomination was given as one reason for the specie increase. The secretary's report informed Congress that the number of pet banks had been reduced to thirty-four by discontinuing the use of banks which formerly provided minor services in connection with the BUS "and by adding no new ones, except where the public interest seemed to render it imperative or expedient." Woodbury believed the major weakness of the first use of state banks as federal depositories (in the years 1811 to 1816) "to have been the multiplication of them to something over one hundred in number." To emphasize the determination of the administration to adhere to these principles Woodbury informed Congress that "the system is now arranged so as probably to require hereafter few changes."[33]

33. *Executive Documents*, 24 Cong., 1 sess., no. 3. Woodbury sent a copy of his letter to the Morris Canal and Banking Company and

Generalizations about Treasury management during the pet banking era cannot be formulated on an analysis of Wall Street banks alone. The fact that a few pet banks were managed conservatively does not in itself materially dispute the argument that the Jacksonians acted irresponsibly in dismantling national monetary controls and pumping the federal funds into a decentralized network of state banks. However, Woodbury's 1835 Treasury report expressed his belief in the present stability of pet bank operations and his confidence in the continuance of banking conservatism through Treasury direction.

The secretary's confidence in pet banks was based upon their creditor relationship to other state banks. His reports to Congress included among pet bank assets the funds due them from other banks and the notes of other banks they held. This bit of verbal juggling allowed the secretary to claim that the ratio between pet banking assets and liabilities hovered around a conservative one to three.[34] The problem here, as Woodbury knew, was that in any emergency the only asset of real value was the specie the bank held in its own vault. He cautioned one of his pet banks in September 1836 that "in a sudden emergency for specie . . . it may seriously suffer unless it shall possess adequate resources in its own vaults."[35] Specie holdings in pet banks did respond to Woodbury's prodding— up from $6.8 million in January 1835 to $11 million in March 1836—[36] and the secretary hoped that additional potential as-

---

to the Bank of America's George Newbold, and referred further applicants to the letter for a full consideration of Treasury policy (Woodbury to Phoenix Bank, Dec. 9, 1835; Woodbury to Southard Bank, Dec. 11, 1835, Letters to Banks).

34. *Senate Documents*, 24 Cong., 1 sess., nos. 313, 379.

35. Woodbury to Westminster Bank, Sept. 10, 1836, Letters to Banks.

36. *Senate Documents*, 24 Cong., 1 sess., nos. 2 and 268.

sets in the form of other bank obligations would see the banks through any crisis.

Woodbury's confidence was misplaced, since debts of other state institutions held by pet banks proved relatively weak assets when public confidence in the banking structure waned; furthermore, Woodbury's efforts to bolster confidence by increasing vault specie generated political opposition that undermined his labors. The economic strength of pet banks, particularly the leading ones on Wall Street, rekindled charges that administration policy was the obedient servant of New York interests. Woodbury's efforts often were unappreciated or misinterpreted even by Democratic stalwarts. The anti-bank bias of Senator Benton led him to listen sympathetically to Woodbury's expansionist critics who argued that the public funds were "hoarded" by Wall Street. Woodbury assured "Bullion" Benton that these charges were groundless and motivated by the self-interest of competing institutions, but the Missouri senator was convinced that the very strength of pet banks indicated by the increased specie holdings was proof of a banking conspiracy against Jacksonian reforms. He warned Woodbury that pet banks "must neither be idle, neutral, nor treacherous, in the contest now waging for the suppression of the gold currency. . . . Will you take them in hand . . . or shall I have to break upon them in the Senate?"[37]

The real Achilles' heel in Woodbury's Treasury operations was in the obligations of other banks held by pet banks. Woodbury's orders to increase specie required pet banks to take in the obligations of other banks in specie; as they did so, they became the new "monsters" in the financial world. Non-

---

37. Woodbury to Benton, Dec. 10, 1835; Benton to Woodbury, Dec. 13, 1835; Benton to Woodbury, Dec. 28, 1835, Woodbury Papers.

pet banks were far more jealous of sister institutions calling on them for specie than they had been of a national bank when it exercised similar power. A New York City correspondent wrote to Biddle one month after Woodbury's order to increase specie, "Our pet banks are very unpopular. The other banks fear and hate them." He advised Biddle that the BUS branch should reduce its loans to protect its specie from the administration's pets.[38] Woodbury was warned by a Philadelphia correspondent the next month of increased money pressure in that city. "It appears that the deposit banks have received orders from the Government to keep on hand at all times one half of their funds in specie." Other banks refused to extend loans, he explained, because of the fear that the government pets would call on them for specie.[39] The administration's specie reserve policy also aroused sectional economic prejudices which had once been directed against the national Bank. State banks in the Southwest were in a precarious position because of their credit expansion in response to the Texas war and recent crop failures. The Treasury's policy required a specie drain out of these banks as their notes were returned from eastern pets. The administration's opponents in Tennessee charged that this practice was deliberately undertaken to favor New York financial interests at the expense of the Southwest.[40]

Woodbury temporarily reversed his deflationary specie policy as a result of the disastrous fire which swept through the New York City financial district in December 1835. Within a month, however, he instructed the New York City pets once

38. R. Lenox to Biddle, Nov. 17, 1835, Biddle Papers.
39. Henry Henry to Woodbury, Dec. 24, 1835, Woodbury Papers.
40. W. Smith to Polk, April 13, 1836, A. Harris to Polk, April 13, 1836, J. Walker to Polk, April 20, 1836, Polk Papers; Union Bank of Tennessee to Woodbury, Apr. 8, 1836, Letters from Banks.

again to increase specie.[41] Biddle, who was attempting to aid
the businesses hard hit by the fire, sharply criticized the
Treasury action. He wrote a New York associate that it
would be good strategy to expose in the press "that while the
Bank of the United States is engaged in lending to the suffer-
ers by the fire, its path should be crossed by the Treasury
order just issued requiring the deposit Banks to increase their
specie; that is to diminish their loans, and make other Banks
do the same. It really appears to me to be as cold hearted a
proceeding as can well be imagined."[42] Whether the administration's policy was "cold-hearted" is one thing; whether it
was financially wise is another. But it does seem clear that
these Treasury orders, with the results described by Biddle,
do not support the claim that more abundant credit was a
major Jacksonian goal.

Woodbury continued to carry out his specie policy during
the early part of 1836, in spite of increasing anxiety over a
tight money market. The Washington *Globe* in January 1836
took notice of the "complaints repeatedly made, that the Deposit Banks did not loan enough," and answered for the administration: "*We believe, if they have erred, it is in loaning
too much.*" A few months later the *Globe* reaffirmed its position: "We believe that the present state of the currency imposes upon the leading deposit banks the obligation of
lessening their loans, calling upon other banks for regular
settlements and payments of balances in specie, and thus give
a check to their too extended operations."[43] The New York
City pets were, of course, in complete agreement with such a
course of action. Campbell P. White counseled Woodbury

41. Woodbury to Mechanics Bank and The Manhattan Company,
Feb. 18, 1836, Letters to Banks.
42. Biddle to R. Blatchford, Feb. 25, 1836, Biddle Papers.
43. Washington *Globe*, Jan. 9, May 10. 1836.

from the city that the only way to stop the attacks on the pet banks was to make them stronger. "If they are obliged to retain *one half* of the public money in specie, and authorized to call upon the other state banks for specie for their balances, when it may become necessary—there is no kind of danger from the reckless course of the panic makers." But White indicated that the New York City pets were under attack "from some of our friends who are opposed to all Banks." Those who were refused loans by the pets were another source of criticism. "No effort seems to be made either by the *Evening Post* or *Times* to defend the Deposit Banks," White lamented.[44]

Resentment against Wall Street's financial dominance was turned into a political attack on the pet banking operations which allegedly supported that power. But, as White's letter indicates, the administration's policy was not enthusiastically endorsed in all quarters of New York City either. In short, the pet banking "experiment" on Wall Street satisfied relatively few interests either in the city or throughout the state and led to demands for a more inflationary money market in New York and around the country. The growing clamor for credit and the charge that the public money was "locked up" in Wall Street vaults under the arbitrary control of the Secretary of the Treasury was translated into political support for the Distribution-Deposit Act of July 1836. This legislation should be considered the means by which Treasury regulation and control of public funds were reversed and dramatic credit expansion made possible, rather than the culmination of a pol-

44. C. P. White to Woodbury, March 26, 1836, Woodbury Papers. The *Evening Post*, a Loco-foco press, advocated "free banking" while the *Times* represented the Conservative wing of the New York Democracy.

icy of credit expansion begun with the removal of deposits.[45]

The Distribution Act necessitated significant alterations in pet banking operations. The law restricted a government deposit in any one bank to an amount not exceeding three-fourths of its capital. The implications of this provision were clear: since additional banks would have to be selected in every state of the Union, the federal funds would no longer be concentrated in the three Wall Street pets and Woodbury's regulatory procedures worked through them would be curtailed. Another provision of the law which reshaped Treasury policy was the charging of interest for the deposits. Woodbury had been able to prod the pets into cooperation with the administration on the grounds that the banks held the public money without paying for the privilege; now that this was no longer the case, bankers would require freer use of the public funds for loans.[46]

No individual regarded distribution with greater alarm than Reuben Whitney. The Washington agent for many of the original pets realized that his value to these banks was based upon his ability to protect them from competition. Now that distribution required Treasury selection of additional banks, Whitney's services appeared less valuable to his employers.

45. Charles G. Sellers, *James K. Polk, Jacksonian*, 231–232. The critics of Treasury policy undoubtedly exaggerated the influence of the federal surplus upon the economy. There were other influences upon bank credit at this time of equal importance in New York and elsewhere. The revenues from the Erie Canal Fund deposited in New York banks were of fundamental importance (Nathan Miller, *The Enterprise of a Free People: Aspects of Economic Development in New York State during the Canal Period, 1792–1838* [Ithaca, N.Y., 1962]). The point stressed here is that Treasury management was peculiarly vulnerable to political manipulation.

46. The Deposit-Distribution Act is printed in *Register of Debates*, 24 Cong., 1 sess., Appendix, xix–xxi.

Even the faithful Girard reassessed its contract with Whitney in the summer of 1836.[47] Although William Lewis was able to persuade the board to continue to employ Whitney, the latter felt the insecurity of his position. He was alarmed at the prospect of pet banking expansion and critical of general financial conditions, which he blamed upon distribution and inept Treasury management by Woodbury. He yearned for a return to the allegedly sound, well regulated pet banks policy under his efficient supervision.[48]

Distribution was a threat to Whitney, but to others it meant the long awaited opportunity to share the public money. Banks from all parts of the country deluged the Treasury with applications for pet bank status. No one exerted greater pressure on the Treasury for additional bank selections than New York and members of the Regency.

The banking expansion required by distribution allowed additional New York banks to be appointed, both in New York City and upstate. New York City's Seventh Ward Bank was presided over by Walter Bowne, a former BUS supporter. He had been converted to the Jacksonian cause in the Bank War and was rewarded with the presidency of the bank, chartered in the spring of 1833.[49] But further favors to the bank in the form of the public deposits were not forthcoming until distribution forced Treasury banking expansion. Bowne reminded Woodbury, shortly before passage of the

47. Whitney's brother, a Philadelphia businessman, had been given unusually large loans from the Girard Bank, which even Whitney conceded was a polite form of blackmail for his Washington influence in keeping large federal deposits in the Philadelphia pet (Whitney to Lewis, Nov. 3, 1836, Lewis-Neilson Papers).

48. McFaul and Gatell, "The Outcast Insider," *Pennsylvania Magazine of History and Biography*, XCI (1967), 132–134.

49. Gatell, "Sober Second Thoughts," *Journal of American History*, LIII (1966), 29–30.

Distribution Act, that the public money was concentrated in the lower part of the city. He pointed to the strategic location of his bank: "Ship builders, steam engine makers, artists, and mechanics generally are better known here than in Wall Street."[50] Others pointed out the bank's political credentials. Churchill Cambreleng, William Marcy and Azariah Flagg supported the bank's application for pet bank status in the summer of 1836, Flagg terming the bank's directors the most "faithful Democrats of the State."[51]

The Bank of Troy in upstate New York was also selected by Woodbury after recommendations from Marcy, Dix, Flagg and Tallmadge.[52] The Secretary at first rejected the application on the grounds that not enough money was collected and disbursed at Troy to justify the selection. Woodbury refused many applications under the provision of the act which prevented the moving of funds from bank to bank unless needed for disbursement and receipt. Since the law indirectly tied pet bank expansion to commercial-governmental transactions, additional Treasury selections were required in New York City, with the result that a large share of the funds would remain on deposit there. Upstate Albany Democrats renewed their pressure on Woodbury to redress this balance by appointing additional pets in Albany. An impressive list of Democrats urged Woodbury to appoint the Albany City Bank and the Canal Bank, also in Albany, but the secretary refused, again on the grounds that not enough money was collected and disbursed there.

While it may have been impossible to satisfy completely

50. Bowne to Woodbury, May 25, 1836, Letters from Banks.
51. Cambreleng to Woodbury, June 21, 1836; Marcy to Woodbury, May 19, 1836; Flagg to Woodbury, May 19, 1836, *ibid*.
52. Marcy, Dix, and Flagg wrote to Woodbury on July 13, 1836; Tallmadge on July 18, 1836 (*ibid*.).

the political-financial interests involved, Woodbury might have handled the New York situation more circumspectly if pet banking had been solely a political engine to advance the Democratic cause in New York and elsewhere. Van Buren had personally recommended the Albany City Bank (it was one of the few times he intervened directly in the Treasury's selection of pet banks) and he was seconded by Senator Silas Wright, as well as Dix, Flagg and Marcy.[53] Similar pressure was exerted in favor of the Canal Bank of Albany.[54] Woodbury's refusal of both banks led Democratic Congressman Aaron Vanderpoel to demand that the secretary submit his objections *"in writing"* for the information of his Albany colleagues.[55] Despite such pressures, Woodbury resolutely adhered to the law's requirements that banks could be chosen only in areas where there was adequate dispersal and collection. Albany Democrats would have to be satisfied with the federal funds on deposit in the Albany Mechanics and Farmers Bank, while the lion's share of the public money for the Empire State remained concentrated in New York City.[56]

Woodbury used another provision of the Distribution Act

53. Van Buren to Woodbury, Sept. 21, 1836; Wright to Woodbury, June 9, 1836; Dix, Flagg and Marcy to Woodbury, July 8, 1836; Erastus Corning to Woodbury, Sept. 22, 1836. Recommendations of Banks.

54. Wright, Dix, and Flagg to Woodbury, July 13, 1836 (*ibid.*).

55. Vanderpoel to Woodbury, Jan. 7, 1837 (*ibid.*).

56. Woodbury's opposition to Regency recommendations was supported by New York Democratic Congressman Ransom H. Gillet. He wrote to Woodbury in August 1836, "I think it probable that you will be applied to select, . . . some of the banks in the central and western, and perhaps northern part of our state. I have reflected some on the subject and arrived at the conclusion, that no good can result to us from the selections of any bank in the state which is under the control of my political friends" (Aug. 12, 1836, Woodbury Papers).

to urge pet banks to increase specie. The act gave the secretary of the Treasury discretionary power to impose specie reserves upon the pet banks. Accordingly, Woodbury ordered all pet bankers to maintain a one-fourth specie reserve against circulation. "The proportion of specie to the actual circulation of a Bank is regarded as one of the most important considerations in view of the safety of its operations," he advised a new pet banker. An inadequate ratio of specie to circulation was sufficient excuse for refusing to appoint new banks under the law, or Woodbury might delay their appointment until he was assured by later returns that their specie was adequate to their circulation.[57]

The Distribution Act was intended by its proponents to serve as an inflationary stimulant to the economy, but Woodbury's specie reserve policy hampered monetary expansion and threatened the preferential position of the original pets. Reuben Whitney vigorously opposed Woodbury's policy. In the fall of 1836 he wrote to his brother-in-law at the Girard Bank: "If it was possible that I could have the power, I could by undoing a part that is done cause a great change in the monetary state of the country."[58] He quarreled openly with Woodbury and even asked the president to intervene. According to Whitney both Benjamin Butler, the attorney general, and Amos Kendall agreed with him, "but you know how difficult it is for one member of the C. to interfere with another department," he lamented to Lewis.[59] Jackson was not at all sympathetic to Whitney's pleas for a more conciliatory

57. Woodbury to York Bank, Oct. 10, 1836; to Lafayette Bank, July 15, 1836; to Bank of River Raisin, July 26, 1836; to Commercial Bank, Sept. 13, 1836; to Merchants and Manufacturers Bank, Aug. 10, 1836; to Cumberland Bank, Aug. 1, 1836; to Franklin Bank, Aug. 2, 1836, Letters to Banks.
58. Whitney to Lewis, Nov. 2, 1836, Lewis-Neilson Papers.
59. Whitney to Lewis, Nov. 4, 1836, *ibid.*

policy toward the banks and did nothing to interfere with Woodbury's Treasury management.

Whitney's disagreement with Treasury management had nothing to do with the administration's hard-money goals. He even supported mild forms of monetary reform and urged them upon pet bankers as essential for remaining in Treasury favor. Again in agreement with Washington, he believed that there had been too much credit expansion throughout 1835 and that restraints were needed. The key to Whitney's quarrel with the Treasury was his increasing inability to impress the secretary with the problems of pet bankers. Distribution necessitated heavy drafts on the original pets to newly appointed banks. With few exceptions, Woodbury did little to alleviate the financial distress caused by such transfers; it was his insistence upon carrying out the letter of the law concerning these withdrawals that prompted Whitney's futile attempts to protect the faithful original pets.

Woodbury justified his refusal to adopt a more flexible distribution policy on the grounds that it had been the financial community which demanded a distribution of the public money, and that it was now reaping the fruits of its own folly. In response to a New York banker's pleas for the department to take some action which would stop the flow of specie from his and other banks, Woodbury replied that he could do nothing: "Congress have in fact voted away from you most of the surplus—and your merchants and banks as a body— with some exceptions . . . are said to have urged the measure and rejoiced at its adoption. I pity their short sighted policy."[60] It was Woodbury's contention that he was only following the dictates of Congress, since the passage of the Distribution Act had reduced his power over the economy of the country.

60. Woodbury to C. P. White, April 7, 1836, Woodbury Papers.

"We are only executive officers as to the laws and must enforce this since it has passed," Woodbury wrote to a friend. "I hope some of the anticipated evil may be averted but I hope without much confidence," he continued, "as the system is now the system of Congress and not of the President and this Department—and Congress is now responsible for its operation."[61]

The Distribution Act prohibited the Treasury from transferring funds from one area of the country to another for the purpose of sustaining credit. This restrictive clause stated that any transfer of funds "for the purpose of accommodating the banks to which the transfer may be made, or to sustain their credit, or for any other purpose whatever, except it be to facilitate the public disbursements, and to comply with the provisions of this act, be, and the same are hereby, prohibited and declared to be illegal."[62] Under these conditions, Woodbury was justified in claiming that Congress had deprived him of his discretionary power over the banking system. The restriction seemed sensible enough to most congressmen and the opposition felt that such a clause implied past Treasury favoritism in bolstering the credit of favored administration pets. Whatever the motivation behind its inclusion in the act, Woodbury used the provsion to justify his refusal to appoint additional banks where insufficient funds were collected (as in Albany) and his denial of aid to those original pets hard hit by the transfer of funds. It was clear that congressional restrictions on Treasury operations angered Woodbury but at the same time eased his responsibility for the national economy.

The new restrictions imposed by Congress impressed the secretary with the importance to the national economy of

61. Woodbury to A. Greenleaf, June 20, 1836, *ibid.*
62. *Register of Debates,* 24 Cong., 1 sess., Appendix, xix–xxi.

Treasury operations. In the fall of 1836, in a letter to the Commercial Bank of Cincinnati, Woodbury analyzed the current relationship between the Treasury and deposit banks: "It does not occupy the position of a central banking institution or one at all analagous, and to which the Deposite Banks stand in relation of Branches; it cannot therefore be governed by many considerations which would be appropriate to that position—but not to that in which I am placed."[63] Woodbury was not engaging in a Jacksonian celebration of the demise of central banking. Rather, now that distribution had limited his discretionary powers, the secretary was contrasting the present situation with the former pet banking system which he had attempted to manage like that of a central bank to branch banks. It had not been Woodbury's conscious intent to transform the Treasury into the focal point of central banking operations. The Jacksonian evolution of banking policy from its early simple emphasis upon specie to later specific controls over credit was made possible through the coincidence of interests among Wall Street pet bankers and increasing Treasury awareness and concern over an unregulated credit structure. To what extent Woodbury might have moved the Washington Treasury into even greater command over banking and credit, if the Distribution Act had not intervened, would have depended upon financial and political considerations. If the overwhelming congressional support for distribution is to be taken as an indication, the chances for greater Treasury responsibility were slim.

The unreliability of the Democratic majority in Congress led to the administration's most forceful executive action on banking and currency, the issuance of the Specie Circular in July 1836. This circular directed government agents to re-

63. Woodbury to Commercial Bank of Cincinnati, Nov. 15, 1836, Letters to Banks.

ceive only gold and silver in payment for public lands after December 1836. The paper money generated by the bank credit expansion increased dangerously under the stimulus of land speculation. The increase of land purchases with bank paper of decreasing value convinced Jackson and others that some restriction on land sales was imperative in order to break the cycle of western land speculation fed by bank credit. Furthermore, the circular was expected to restrict banking expansion throughout the country. Reuben Whitney enthusiastically supported the measure, which indicates that its appeal reached beyond the zealous hard-money enthusiasts around Jackson. Within the Treasury there was particular concern over the banking practices in the Southwest, specifically their extended note issues in relation to specie. The Specie Circular forced these banks to reduce their loans and increase vault holdings.[64]

Even though the circular fell within the area of Treasury authority, Woodbury apparently had little to do with the decision to issue it. He later wrote to a friend that the measure was not his and added, "I have always differed even from its foes as well as friends in my estimate of its importance for either good or evil."[65] This was not a very forceful position for the man who had primary responsibility for the public money and its influence on bank credit. Woodbury's neutrality contrasted with Benton's insistence that the Treasury take action. In April 1836, three months before the appearance of the circular, Benton introduced in the Senate a resolution calling for exclusive specie payments for land. The

64. John Niles to Welles, June 23, 1836, Welles Papers; Whitney to Lewis, Aug. 22, Nov. 2, 1836, Lewis-Neilson Papers; Woodbury to Union Bank of Tennessee, Aug. 5, 1836, Letters to Banks.
65. J. King to Woodbury, April 21, 1837; Woodbury to King, April 21, 1837, Woodbury Papers.

resolution was quickly dismissed by a Senate long familiar with the Missouri Senator's obsession with gold; he seemed confident, nevertheless, that action eventually would be taken, predicting that "whether his proposition became law or not, it must take effect. The Secretary of the Treasury would have to do by regulation what he proposed that Congress should do by law."[66] The accuracy of Benton's prediction demonstrated to such Democratic senators as Rives and Tallmadge that his anti-banking views were still closest to those of the executive.

The combined effect of distribution and the Specie Circular was to increase dramatically the pressure upon banks' specie reserves. The transfers of public money required by distribution were made more difficult by Woodbury's insistence that all pet banks maintain a conservative specie reserve ratio against circulation. The secretary's instructions drove pet bankers to take in their credit with other banks in specie, or at least provided a convenient excuse for them to do so. One New York City pet called upon another for $50,000 in specie, insisting that it was forced to take this action because of Woodbury's pressure to increase vault holdings.[67] An Ohio pet banker complained to Woodbury that the most harmful specie transfers under the Distribution Act were not to distant parts of the country, in accordance with the normal channels of trade, but to neighboring banks.[68] This interbank scramble for specie further endangered an already precarious banking structure. A fellow New Yorker urged Van Buren to have Woodbury "delay at least for a few days all agitation

66. *Register of Debates*, 24 Cong., 1 sess., 1254–1259.

67. Mechanics Bank to Woodbury, March 24, 1837, Letters from Banks.

68. Commercial Bank of Cincinnati to Woodbury, Oct. 15, 1836, *ibid.*

on the subject of the amount of specie in the Deposit Banks but leave matters to take their course."[69]

Woodbury did delay some large drafts on the Wall Street pets. The *Globe*, however, attacked any Treasury accommodation of the banks as political heresy. While Woodbury was engaged in crucial negotiations with Wall Street bankers, the *Globe* thundered: "We hope and trust that the government will stand to its course—carry the Distribution law into effect, though it should swamp all the banks in New York. These banks and their managers set the measure afloat, and supported it—make them drink their own mixture to the dregs."[70]

The traditional Jacksonian mistrust of the association between government and banking was increased by the impact of distribution upon Treasury actions. The *Globe* bemoaned the fact that distribution required governmental decisions which significantly affected credit in various parts of the country. It was easy for the fiery Jacksonian editor to slip back into the conventional rhetoric of laissez faire: "If Government is to be engaged in the money market, and by its action make money scarce or plenty, and change the prices of things, by throwing its weight into this or that scale, it becomes like the Bank of the United States Government, a great system to foster gambling and speculation, instead of the regular business and industry of the country." Blair advocated an end to the connection between government and banking through reduced government revenue.[71]

Woodbury reactivated the Jacksonian concept of state legislative restrictions on banking in his annual report for Decem-

69. T. Phelps to Van Buren, April 20, 1837, Van Buren Papers.
70. Washington *Globe*, Oct. 24, 1836. Woodbury reportedly urged Blair repeatedly to cease his attacks on state banks (Nathaniel Niles to Rives, June 8, 1837, Rives Papers).
71. Washington *Globe*, Nov. 24, 1836.

ber 1836; warning of the danger from increasing paper money stimulated by distribution, he urged the states to impose a one-third specie reserve against bank circulation as well as a limit on discounts in accordance with a bank's capital and deposits. Clearly discouraged by the problems of Treasury regulation and the ease with which Congress could interfere, Woodbury concluded that if the states would impose strict regulations on banks with periodic legislative examinations then banking could be thrown open to all.[72] Free access to a business carefully regulated by public authority was gaining in popularity among Jacksonians attempting to solve the dilemma of banking and politics.

The Treasury management of the public money was a result of the political situation described in the previous chapter. Woodbury's stewardship of the pet banking system clearly demonstrates that the administration's "experiment" was more than a Jacksonian political device or a federal abandonment of public controls over the economy. He and other Jacksonians were in the uncomfortable position of recognizing the need for national economic regulation but always meeting such needs reluctantly and apologetically, lest their actions validate the Whig contention that the restraints of a national bank were necessary. The Jacksonians' goal was economic stability through increased use of specie, the impersonal and natural regulator, which they hoped to achieve by the means of temporary governmental regulation. But eventually the means became the end and Woodbury privately defended his actions on the grounds that he was performing the same functions as the dreaded "Monster" BUS. In such a situation, perhaps even Woodbury welcomed the Distribution Act as a reprieve from responsibilities which he found so alien.

72. *Senate Documents*, 24 Cong., 2 sess., no. 2.

Things had gone too far to conceal much longer the wide divergence between Democratic practice and theory regarding banking. Conservative Democrats, angered by Woodbury's distribution policies and insulted by the issuance of the Specie Circular, planned to reverse Washington policy by openly challenging these anti-bank actions. Hard-money Democrats were only too willing to meet the challenge and to attribute Conservative defense of banks to the corrupting nexus between banking and government.

7

Jacksonians "Divorce" the Banks

The emergence of the Conservative insurgents as a distinct
political group within the Democratic party fully revealed
the divergent tendencies toward banking among Jacksonians
and finally thwarted the Van Buren administration's original
plan for establishing an independent treasury. In retrospect
the Conservative movement appears suicidal, like most unsuccessful minority actions; bad timing and unforeseen circumstances contributed as much as anything to its downfall.
Conservatives attempted to redirect Democratic policy before the bank suspension of 1837 and were caught in the ensuing financial emergency. They had taken a resolute stand
in defense of state banks, the credit system, and mild currency
reform, but the daring "experiment" of 1834 was doomed to
appear as something quite different in 1837. Unable to initiate
party policy, Conservatives consoled themselves with the belief that they held the balance of power between administration Democrats and challenging Whigs. To retain their
political influence, however, it was necessary that the banking
issue remain in conflict; once resolved, by the creation of
either an independent treasury or a new national bank, Conservative strength would diminish.

Working most effectively on the perimeter of the party,

Conservatives attracted supporters on specific issues dealing with banks and the currency. The leadership they exerted in the struggle over the Distribution Act is a good example of the balance of power held by the Conservatives. Far from embarrassed by this legislation, their leaders, Rives and Tallmadge, promoted distribution to the level of a political philosophy. Their speeches in defense of the measure made it clear that their faction of the Democratic party stood for decentralized credit expansion based upon federal-state cooperation. They called, first, for the federal government to remain frugal and true to orthodox Republican principles by pumping its funds back in to state banks, and secondly, for the states to cooperate by restricting low-denomination bank note circulation. The twin dangers of the Whig national bank and Benton's hard-money extremism were thus avoided by the Conservative program.

Conservative success in the distribution controversy was eclipsed, however, by the issuance of the Specie Circular, which threatened to check the economic expansion promised by distribution. Conservative-leaning Democrats feared that support for the Specie Circular would become a new test of Jacksonian allegiance. Though the issuance of the circular did demonstrate Benton's influence with Jackson, the overwhelming majority for distribution in the previous session of Congress attested to the strength of Conservative sentiment. Consequently, Conservatives hoped to turn the second or short session of the Twenty-fourth Congress into a ratifying body for their philosophy of governmental finance. Their goals were to impress both the retiring Jackson and the newly elected Van Buren with their strength within the party and to halt the spread of Benton's anti-bank extremism.

Silas Wright wrote to his New York ally Azariah Flagg of his concern about impending Democratic actions in the Congress convening in December 1836. He feared there were insufficient Democratic votes to maintain Jackson's Specie Circular and attributed the lack of support to extensive land speculation among Democratic members of Congress. The circular caught many Democrats in "an unguarded hour," Wright confided to Flagg.[1]

Fears about the political future of the Democratic party and the personal financial speculations of many of its members created considerable pressure on Democratic leadership committed to the Specie Circular. Whigs everywhere opposed it and were ready to join with Democratic insurgents to repeal it. The circular further alienated other elements already resentful toward the administration for using the Distribution Act as an excuse to implement what they considered absurd anti-banking practices. Nowhere was the anti-administration line publicized with greater force and consistency than in the pages of the New York *Journal of Commerce*. The *Journal* was theoretically apolitical except when political action threatened to disrupt the commercial interests to which the paper was devoted. It had taken a mild anti-BUS position, criticizing Biddle for his retrenchment after the removal of federal funds, and was consistently in favor of additional banking capital for New York City.[2] The Specie Circular threatened New York City interests by draining its specie for western use, and the *Journal* reprimanded the President for this injustice to the city. Referring to Jackson as the "General" to emphasize his martial disregard of Congress, the paper declared that the circular would not stop speculation anyway ("So would a feather beat back a hurricane"). The problem,

1. Wright to Flagg, Dec. 16, 1836, Flagg Papers.
2. Blair considered the *Journal* an opposition paper and republished its editorials criticizing BUS retrenchment (Washington *Globe*, Nov. 30, 1833; New York *Journal of Commerce*, Nov. 7, 1835).

as the *Journal* saw it, was that "a strange love of gold and silver has seized upon our President" causing him to impose his fanaticism upon the country "under the false opinion that the wealth and strength of a Bank consists in the specie deposited in its vaults."[3] The editorials of the *Journal of Commerce* demonstrate that Jacksonians did not have a monopoly on the rhetoric of laissez faire: "We do not elect a President to control speculation in land. We have not submitted to the degradations of permitting government to investigate and direct the affairs of private business. . . . Is it any of his business that the people speculate?"[4] Even before the disruptions caused by distribution and the Specie Circular, the *Journal* stated its creed succinctly: "The best and only safe regulator of the currency is a good and free system, left in its movements to the discretion and sagacity of business men."[5]

Conservative Jacksonians were not so willing to abandon banking regulation to the wisdom of Wall Streeters. In the second session of the Twenty-fourth Congress, Conservatives allowed the Whigs to make the first move against the Specie Circular; as expected, Senator Thomas Ewing introduced a resolution calling for outright repeal.[6] Webster, in subsequent debate, declared that the public had a right to know what course the Van Buren administration would pursue on this matter, proclaiming action by the present Congress a test vote of future policy.[7] Rives seized the opportunity to exert Conservative leadership, establishing his Democratic credentials by rejecting the Whig resolution as a censure of the retiring

3. New York *Journal of Commerce*, Oct. 7, 1836; *Journal of Commerce*, Oct. 14, 1836.

4. New York *Journal of Commerce*, Oct. 21, 1836.

5. New York *Journal of Commerce*, Jan. 28, 1835.

6. *Senate Journal*, 24 Cong., 2 sess., 165–66; *Register of Debates*, 24 Cong., 2 sess., 8–17.

7. *Ibid.*, 91.

Jackson. It was the duty of the legislature to make laws, Rives declared, not rescind executive action. He offered instead a measure he claimed was neither rash nor imprudent but would enlarge the specie base of the country. Rives' substitute bill would allow the government to continue to receive all bank notes until 1841, when a prohibition on the governmental receipt of the notes of banks issuing bills under $20 denomination would take effect. It was Rives' plan to combine currency reform with repeal of the circular. The popularity of Rives' position was vividly demonstrated when his bill passed the Senate by an overwhelming vote of forty-one to five.[8]

The restrictions in this legislation would have sharply curtailed small-note circulation, since all banks wanted their paper taken by the government; in this sense it went further than many Jacksonians would have been willing to go a few years earlier. Senator Tallmadge and his Conservative followers did not want any restrictions on bank notes, nor did most of the Whigs, but both groups realized they would have to compromise if the circular was to be repealed at all.

In the House, the Senate bill passed by a vote of 143 to 59,[9] but House Democrats were sharply divided. All fifty-nine votes to retain the circular were Democratic, while another fifty-four Democrats joined House Whigs in support of Rives' bill. The vote fell into a somewhat sectional pattern in that Democrats from the South, Southeast, and far West either voted overwhelmingly for repeal or abstained. The new states of Arkansas and Michigan had one congressman apiece, both Democrats and both voting for repeal. The one Democrat in the House from Louisiana abstained. The two-man Democratic delegation from Mississippi voted for the repeal, as did the only two Democrats from Alabama. Of the six

8. *Ibid.*, 120–123; *Senate Journal*, 24 Cong., 2 sess., 165–166, 235–236.
9. *House Journal*, 24 Cong., 2 sess., 557–558.

Democrats from Georgia, two voted for repeal and four abstained.

Party organization was fluid in Indiana and Illinois, and their congressmen voted against the administration. Illinois had three seats in the House, all Democratic, and all three congressmen voted for repeal. Six of the seven-man delegation from Indiana were Democrats, but three of them voted for repeal and three abstained. In Ohio political parties were much more sharply defined and the hard-money aims of the Jacksonians clearly spelled out. Eight of the nineteen Ohio congressmen were Democrats and five voted against repeal.

The administration gained most of its votes against the circular's repeal from the East, mainly the Northeast, but again there were differences within this sectional alignment attributable to state political organizations. Maine, a strong Democratic state, supplied six votes against repeal. Of the five congressmen from New Hampshire, all Democrats, four voted against repeal while one abstained. But in the sister state of Connecticut, where the Democrats were more divided, there was less unity in the voting. Of the six Democrats from Connecticut, only one voted against repeal, three abstained, and two voted for repeal.

New York Jacksonians supplied the strongest hard-money support for the administration. New York's congressional delegation included thirty-one Democrats and nine Whigs. Twenty-five of the Democrats voted to maintain the circular, only two voted for repeal, and four abstained. This vote was an unusual display of party discipline and fidelity to the hard-money aims of the administration, considering the repeated allegation that the circular drained New York's specie to pay for western land. A significant break in Democratic ranks occurred within the Virginia delegation. Of the sixteen Virginia House Democrats, only three voted against repeal, three abstained, and ten voted for repeal. Sensitivity over executive usurpation accounted for the adverse vote among the Virginia Democrats. Led by Thomas Ritchie of the Richmond *Enquirer,* they regarded the exercise of presidential power with suspicion, particularly when it resulted in their bank notes no longer being received by government land offices.

The fifty-nine House Democrats who voted against repeal of the Specie Circular were motivated in part by party discipline and in part by an ingrained anti-bank position. The fifty-nine Democrats in the preceeding (Twenty-third) Congress all had identical voting records in support of the administration on roll calls dealing with the Bank of the United States, deposit removal, the deposit bill, and the Binney amendment. When they divided on the Specie Circular vote many Democrats simply chose what they considered the alternative most consistent with their hard-money views. Twenty-seven of the Democrats who voted against repeal of the Specie Circular were among those thirty-eight Democrats who had voted against distribution earlier. The holdovers from this group who sat in the Twenty-fifth Congress with one exception voted with the administration on the independent treasury bill and other measures considered to be against the banking interests.

The Conservative plan for repealing the Specie Circular while still retaining the original hard-money aims of the administration failed when Jackson pocket-vetoed the bill. Silas Wright, noting the "peculiar interest" some of his colleagues had in the bill, had advised the president to put the bill "to sleep" rather than return it with a veto which was sure to be overridden by Congress.[10] The Rives-Tallmadge faction once again found itself in command of Congress but without

10. Wright to Benjamin Butler, undated, Wright Papers.

power within administration councils. Nevertheless, they were convinced that the newly elected Van Buren would be more responsive to the will of the people as that will was demonstrated by congressional action. Confident that it spoke for a majority of Democrats, the Conservative leadership laid plans to establish its own Washington newspaper, the *Madisonian*, to counteract the anti-bank views of the *Globe*.[11]

As Jackson retired to the Hermitage, pressure was put on Van Buren, as president, either to repeal or to modify the Specie Circular. The New York *Journal of Commerce* predicted that the circular's repeal would be one of the first acts of the new administration. Van Buren's mail increased sharply, with most of his correspondents favoring either a direct repeal or some modification of the circular. Van Buren wrote to Jackson in March that "every mail brings me bundles of letters, and memorials from our friends in favor of rescinding the Treasury order."[12] The tone of the letter suggests that Van Buren was inviting the former president to say that some sort of modification would be acceptable to him; however, the letter is incomplete and may never have been sent. Van Buren solicited the opinions of his closest advisers, but decided against Cabinet discussion because he knew it would be sharply divided.[13] Conservative Senators Rives and Tallmadge assured Van Buren that without repeal the next Congress would oppose his administration.[14]

Wherever Van Buren turned, sentiment appeared to favor

11. Thomas Allen to W. C. Rives, March 14, 1837, Rives Papers.

12. Van Buren to Jackson, March 1837, Van Buren Papers. For a recent analysis of the troubled Van Buren presidency see James C. Curtis, *The Fox at Bay: Martin Van Buren and the Presidency, 1837–1841* (Lexington, Ky., 1970).

13. Memorandum, March 24, 1837, Van Buren Papers.

14. Tallmadge to Van Buren, March 15, 1837; Rives to Van Buren, April 7, 1837, *ibid.*

a repeal of the Specie Circular. "If you cannot turn the storm, bend to it," the new President was advised by Thomas Cooper of South Carolina.[15] Among Van Buren's closest advisers, only Cambreleng and Flagg took a strong stand in favor of retaining the circular, while Silas Wright, though he also favored it, was agreeable to some modification.[16]

Although political realism seemed to dictate otherwise, Van Buren's commitment to Jacksonian principles required him to support the circular and the anti-banking position it represented, regardless of the consequences. A long-standing belief that his popularity among the people depended upon his undeviating adherence to Jacksonian ideals made repeal of Jackson's directive tantamount to political betrayal. The New York *Journal of Commerce* explained to its readers in May 1837 that the repeal was delayed because Van Buren "feared the consequences of taking ground at so early a period of his administration in opposition to his political godfather."[17] Van Buren, having reaped the rewards of being the Jacksonian heir-apparent, was discovering that such a role had drawbacks as well.

Van Buren was certainly equal to the task of finding some sort of modification of the Treasury circular while preserving the Jacksonian goals of currency reform. A few such modifications were discussed but never seriously pursued.[18] Van Buren believed that any changes in the circular would act as a psychological stimulus for credit expansion (the opponents

15. Cooper to Van Buren, Apr. 14, 1837, *ibid.*
16. Cambreleng to Van Buren, April 8, 1837; Flagg to Van Buren, April 10, 1837; Wright to Van Buren, March 21, 1837, *ibid.*
17. Nathaniel Niles to W. C. Rives, June 13, 1837, Rives Papers; New York *Journal of Commerce,* May 2, 1837.
18. C. P. White to Van Buren, March 14, 1837; Silas Wright to Van Buren, March 21, 1837, Van Buren Papers.

of the circular favored repeal for this reason) and would particularly endanger banking operations in the inflation-prone West and Southwest.[19] These economic considerations were not merely rationalizations for a political course he felt he must follow; some of the more conservative bankers of the Southwest shared the same view. Thomas Fletcher, a former director of the BUS Nashville branch and more recently director of the Planters Bank of Tennessee, informed Van Buren that the Specie Circular checked speculation in land and other illegitimate uses of credit. The circular, according to this banker, would "purify and cleanse the foul spirit of speculation which still exists among us."[20] The president of the Commercial Bank of New Orleans agreed. He felt that the cumulative effect of the circular would be to force all banks to contract their loans and lay in specie. If some of the banks had to close their doors, he would not be distressed: "The *bursting* of a few of these large Houses . . . will yet in my opinion produce a salutary change in business affairs here and cause greater caution on the part of our Banks."[21]

The financial impact of the Distribution Act upon the banks had been taken by anti-banking Democrats as an indication of banking instability. The same phenomenon was even more apparent in Jacksonian statements regarding the effect of the Specie Circular on the banking system. Silas Wright assured Van Buren that the circular would help "to bring all those speculations to the test of truth and fact by arresting credits to all which rest upon credit, and transfer the cash capital of the country to the uses of legitimate business of the country."[22]

19. Van Buren to W. C. Rives, April 8, 1837, *ibid.;* Woodbury to N. West, April 14, 1837, Woodbury Papers.
20. Fletcher to Van Buren, March 28, 1837, Van Buren Papers.
21. G. Hewes to Woodbury, March 24, 1837, Woodbury Papers.
22. Wright to Van Buren, March 21, 1837, Van Buren Papers.

The *Globe* firmly stated its analysis of the circular's effects: "Good banks will not be shocked, and bad ones ought to be."[23] Thus the more zealous anti-banking Jacksonians dismissed all subsequent pleas for relief as the anguished cries of speculators.

The public had begun to interpret the Specie Circular as governmental confirmation of Jacksonian suspicions about banking unreliability. "I found the people excited," a western banker reported to Woodbury. "They appear to distrust all Banks, they think Govt. has no confidence in them." Biddle concurred. His letter to an English banking house in April 1837 stated that there was plenty of specie in the country to carry on business, but the policies of the government had made it unavailable to the banks. "The Crusade against the Banks," as Biddle called it, had caused a drain on specie which forced them to curtail loans sharply. Shortly after the suspension of specie payments one of Van Buren's correspondents blamed the Specie Circular for the situation which he claimed "struck at the very vital of public confidence. It was saying to the people, beware of the Banks. They are in a ticklish position; they are not to be trusted."[24] Banks were experiencing an unusually heavy drain on their specie reserves. "Our canal hands here refuse to take any of our state paper," one westerner reported, "except such as is on our branch that they can go and draw the specie." By mid-April, a New Yorker told Van Buren that "the fate of this commercial community is now as it were suspended by a thread, all confidence is at an end." A week later another New Yorker informed the president that there was a "quiet run" on the

23. Washington *Globe*, July 12, 1836.
24. Franklin Bank of Cincinnati to Woodbury, Sept. 12, 1836, Letters from Banks; Biddle to Baring Brothers, April 1, 1837, Biddle Papers; P. Lindsley to Van Buren, June 1, 1837, Van Buren Papers.

banks in New York City. Within two weeks all the banks in the country closed their doors.[25]

The Jacksonian preference for specie over paper money was turned into a public vote of no confidence in all notes and in the banks which issued them. The people threatened eventually to run the banks' specie reserves down to the vault floor, rather than accept bank notes. A revolution in the currency of the country had been achieved, not gradually and with the assistance of the banks as Jacksonians had planned, but dramatically and with disastrous effects. Many Democrats believed that the banks had failed the country, that any attempt at future government-bank cooperation would be useless, and that the only solution was for the government to divorce itself from banking altogether.

The collapse of the banking system in May 1837 caused Conservatives, now thrown on the defensive by the apparent "proof" of state bank unreliability, to alter their course. It was one thing to defend a system that was functioning, however imperfectly, and quite another to advocate the re-establishment as government agents of those bankers who allegedly betrayed the public trust by suspending specie payments. Furthermore, the general bank suspension polarized Democrats and Whigs around the separate issues of the independent treasury and the national bank, while the Conservatives continued to defend the discredited state banks.[26] Whereas

25. C. Fletcher to J. Tipton, Dec. 21, 22, 1836, in Nellie A. Robertson and Dorothy Riker, eds., *The John Tipton Papers* (3 vols.; Indianapolis, 1942), III, 330–331; T. Phelps to Van Buren, April 20, 1837, Enos Throop to Van Buren, April 29, 1837, Van Buren Papers.

26. Governor William L. Marcy opposed the independent treasury but reluctantly supported the measure when the administration committed itself (Marcy to P. Wetmore, June 29, 1838, Marcy Papers; Ivor D. Spencer, *The Victor and the Spoils: A Life of William L. Marcy* [Providence, 1959], 93–95).

Conservatives had formerly worked within Democratic ranks in drawing off the moderates from Benton's leadership, the only opportunity now open to them was a direct alliance with Whigs in opposition to an independent treasury.

Conservatives were moving on to more dangerous ground, but their leaders probably reasoned that they had little to lose. Both Rives and Tallmadge felt they had been outmaneuvered for positions of leadership within the Democratic party. Rives had long been irritated by what he considered the overbearing party discipline and the policy of rewards based upon party fidelity. His extravagant speeches in the Senate in favor of hard money (which cost him his Senate seat) were warmly applauded by Jackson and the Jacksonians generally. Nonetheless his hopes for the vice-presidency in 1836 were crushed when the Van Burenites chose the brawling frontiersman, Richard Johnson of Kentucky. Furthermore, he found that the hard-money issue was better represented in the Senate by "Bullion" Benton. Despite Rives' speeches, his faithful service and many talents, the Virginia Senator continued to be merely the lieutenant to Benton, the general of the hard-money crusade.[27]

Tallmadge's ambitions were also frustrated by party hierarchy. He operated on a secondary level of the Albany Regency, in the shadow of the prestigious and influential Silas

27. Among many such comments is the following of Rives to a close friend requesting his aid in securing a government appointment: "The truth is that the avenues to Executive favor here are so entirely forestalled by persons resting their claims on *Party considerations* of one sort or another that there is no chance for one, whose pretensions rest on the solid ground of personal merit" (Rives to Nathaniel Niles, March 4, 1833, Nathaniel Niles Papers). Rives was mentioned as a possible vice-presidential candidate before the 1832 election but recognized Van Buren's superior claim (Rives to Van Buren, Oct. 25, 1831, Van Buren Papers).

Wright. Furthermore, as the Democratic crusade moved steadily in the direction of a firmer anti-bank stance, there were others within Regency councils who were better suited and certainly more enthusiastic than Tallmadge. Like Rives, Tallmadge found opportunities for Democratic leadership closed except to those best able to articulate and represent the party's ever increasing anti-banking position.[28]

Politically, it became more and more difficult to distinguish a Conservative Democrat from a Whig, as both stoutly defended the credit system against administration policy. The Whigs still championed a national bank for the nation's economic ills, but they also believed the most immediate task was to prevent the passage of an independent treasury bill. Upon this point Whigs and Conservatives could agree. Rives' ally, Democratic Governor David Campbell of Virginia, was informed that his views were strongly supported by Tennessee Whigs. "They gloss over your opposition to a US Bank, and close upon your views in relation to the subtreasury, and the beneficial effects of the credit system."[29]

Differences in the positions of the two leaders of the movement created tensions among Conservatives. Rives could not work as easily with Virginia Whigs as could Tallmadge with his former New York opponents because the issue of a national bank was of much greater importance to Virginians

28. Tallmadge's actions were rumored to be part of a "design to strengthen Tallmadge and weaken Wright and to smooth the way of the former to the Executive chair" (Marcy to Wetmore, July 20, 1837, Marcy Papers). Two different studies of New York Democratic political leadership indicate the relative unimportance of Tallmadge by a conspicuous omission of his name: Robert V. Remini, "The Albany Regency," *New York History*, XXXIX (1958), 341–355; and Ivor D. Spencer, "William L. Marcy Goes Conservative," *Mississippi Valley Historical Review*, XXXI (1944), 205–224.

29. J. Campbell to D. Campbell, Jan. 19, 1838, Campbell Papers.

than to New Yorkers.[30] Referring to a national bank, Rives wrote in his private correspondence about the "dangerous scheme of a powerful and overshadowing national institution," while Tallmadge avoided the subject. Rives' plan was to continue to use state banks as the only real alternative to a national bank.[31]

Rives and Tallmadge disagreed over Jacksonian monetary reforms as well. Rives had championed the Jacksonian drive to eliminate small-denomination bank notes after the removal of the deposits; his support for currency reform was calculated to satisfy important Virginia interests. The state's banks concentrated along the eastern seaboard were threatened by numerous demands for banks in the state's western areas. Democratic banking interests in Richmond were anything but converts to the virtues of hard coin, but the national Jacksonian crusade against the excesses of paper money tied in with their position favoring moderate banking expansion, preferably in the form of branches under the control of the powerful Richmond Bank of Virginia. Rives' long-standing support for hard money was therefore applauded by his state's banking community as well as his zealous anti-banking constituents.[32]

Tallmadge was faced with a different situation in New York. The hard-money, anti-bank advocates in that state were either in the third party Loco-foco group or in well estab-

---

30. Fellow Senator John Niles wrote of Rives: "He is not in the situation of Tallmadge; the Virginia Whigs will not sustain him" (Niles to Welles, Feb. 22, 1837, Welles Papers).

31. Rives to D. Campbell, May 22, 1837, Campbell Papers.

32. Starnes, *Branch Banking in Virginia*, 61–62. Bank of Virginia president, John Brockenbrough, warned the state legislature that the mixed currency of specie and bank notes would be threatened by an expansion in the number of banks (*Journal of the House of Delegates*, 1834–1835, Doc. no. 23).

lished positions of Regency leadership. Tallmadge appealed to those who wanted a dramatic credit expansion based upon federal aid to the beleagured banks in the form of government deposits and unqualified receipt of their bank notes for government dues. Tallmadge informed Rives in the summer of 1837 that New York Conservatives agreed with the Virginian's strategy of calling for an immediate repeal of the Specie Circular and continued use of state banks as federal depositories. He added, however, that his New York supporters "do not like the provision as to the $10 and $20 notes . . . they think all that better be omitted." Unable to abandon his support for currency reform without appearing blatantly inconsistent to his Virginia constituents, Rives, aided by Governor Campbell, convinced Tallmadge that currency reform was a necessary part of Conservative plans to resume pet banking operations.[33]

Despite their differences, Conservatives were united in opposition to the administration's independent treasury proposal. Realizing that their success on this front would discredit the Benton anti-banking Democrats as party leaders, Conservatives subsequently intended to lead a Democratic-Whig coalition supporting Rives' plan for a renewed pet banks system. They hoped to convince fellow Democrats that their proposal was the only feasible alternative to a national bank and to persuade Whigs that pet banking was preferable to the administration's plan for an independent treasury.

Van Buren's advocacy of an independent treasury in 1837 is more significant than either the bill's abortive passage in 1840 or its final triumph in 1846.[34] It has therefore drawn the

33. Tallmadge to Rives, June 30, 1837; Campbell to Rives, July 17, 1837; Rives to Campbell, Aug. 26, 1837, Campbell Papers.

34. David Kinley, *The Independent Treasury of the United States and Its Relations to the Banks of the Country* (Washington, 1910);

attention of Jacksonian scholars. Arthur Schlesinger, Jr., describes Van Buren's proposal as the logical culmination of Jacksonian banking policy: the government's refusal to accept bank notes lessened the influence of banks over the currency, moderated the economy generally, prevented the further redistribution of wealth from agrarian to financial interests, and politically represented the power of the people over the interests of the business community. These issues were understood perfectly at that time, according to Schlesinger: "The divorce of bank and state represented primarily—both for friends and foes—a further extension of the hard-money policy."[35]

The independent treasury proposal is described by Bray Hammond, in his assault on the theories of Schlesinger and other pro-Jackson historians, as a masterpiece of strategy by the politically astute Van Buren. Hammond portrays Van Buren, in the aftermath of the 1837 Panic, uneasily presiding over a Democratic party divided between state bank interests and zealous anti-bank forces. The latter were encouraged by his predecessor's insistent demands for a governmental hard line against banks. Van Buren could repudiate neither the pro-banking forces within the party which he represented, nor the anti-bank sentiments typified by Jackson.[36] But it was not beyond Van Buren's powers to handle this political situation, according to Hammond. The new president's independent treasury recommendation was a "masterly fusion of the ingenious and obscure. . . . It breathed the sound and fury

Charles G. Sellers, *James K. Polk Continentalist, 1843–1846* (Princeton, 1966), 340–345, 468–470. For a recent study of the independent treasury controversy during Van Buren's presidency see Curtis, *The Fox at Bay*, chs. 4–7.

35. Schlesinger, *Age of Jackson*, 227–229, 239–241.
36. Hammond, *Banks and Politics*, 490.

of Loco-foco distrust of banks but in substance proposed a course of action which subjected them to nothing worse than being called hard names."[37] Thus Hammond describes the Van Buren proposal as nothing more than a partial restriction on state bank notes in return for the complete withdrawal of governmental regulation of banking, a small price for bankers to pay, he argues, since banks were relying more and more on extending credit through deposit creation rather than through bank note issue.

If the independent treasury would prove a help rather than a hindrance to banking operations, why was there so much opposition to the proposal within banking circles? Hammond insists that bankers were just as confused as the anti-bank Loco-focos; moreover, Loco-foco support for the measure convinced suspicious bankers that the independent treasury must be against their interests. In his account, Hammond concludes that Van Buren's political skills were too sophisticated and the entrepreneurial designs of the independent treasury too well concealed for bankers to perceive.[38]

Van Buren's advocacy of an independent treasury represented neither the last step in the Jacksonian design of hard-money radicalism nor another example of Jacksonian fidelity to laissez-faire principles. The Gouge plan for an independent treasury had been drawn up before the Panic of 1837 and had been discussed within administration circles, but this does not mean that its endorsement in 1837 was the culmination of Jacksonian hard-money policy. Abuse of the banking community was integral to Democratic anti-banking rhetoric, eventually resulting in a preference for separation of government from banking; however, the political course of Benton and other zealous anti-bank Democrats illustrates the ability

37. *Ibid.,* 496.   38. *Ibid.,* 496–499.

of Democratic lambs to lie down with financial lions. The argument that the independent treasury was the logical culmination of Jacksonian banking policy originated with Democratic critics who claimed that the Van Buren proposal proved long-standing and deep-seated hostility to all banks. The anti-bank Democrats, embarrassed by their past connections with banks, happily agreed with this interpretation. Thus the *Democratic Review* in October 1837, with the wisdom of hindsight, dismissed the pet banking experiment as a "period of transition, though . . . but few rightly understood it as such."[39]

Van Buren's recommendation of an independent treasury was contingent upon the collapse of the pet banking system; it is ludicrous to believe, as suggested by some administration critics, that the Democrats perpetrated the bank suspension in 1837 in order to clear the way for an independent treasury.[40] This argument should be put in the same category as Jackson's contention that the suspension of specie payments was part of a conspiratorial bargain between Biddle and English financiers.[41] The evidence indicates that Van Buren intended to continue to use state banks in the hope of appeasing both the Benton anti-bank Democrats and the Tallmadge-Rives Conservatives. While this course had its political hazards, it was safer than complete abandonment of state banks.

Furthermore, Van Buren's independent treasury proposal was not a hastily contrived political maneuver, breathing Loco-foco fire while promising laissez-faire action, as Hammond believes. It is true that the thunderous rhetoric which accompanied the recommendation eased the anxieties of anti-

39. *United States Democratic Review*, I (Oct., 1837), 120–122.
40. Hugh Lawson White, *Memoir*, 309–314.
41. Jackson to Moses Dawson, May 26, 1837; Jackson to Amos Kendall, May 26, 1837, Jackson Papers.

bank Democrats, but it is important to note that the administration was not proposing a withdrawal of federal responsibilities for banking. As will be shown later, the Van Buren-sponsored plan actually would have increased the federal responsibility for state banking operations.

Misunderstandings in connection with Van Buren's proposal for an independent treasury were the result of two faulty assumptions about the role of specie. First, it was assumed that independent treasury operations would require exclusive specie payments to the government. Secondly, it was assumed that the only bank regulation possible under an independent treasury operation would be the governmental insistence upon specie payments.

It was not unreasonable to assume that the government would require exclusive specie payments, since such a provision had been associated with former proposals for an independent treasury. This assumption was strengthened when Calhoun, an open advocate of hard money, announced his intention to support the independent treasury proposal.[42] Furthermore, because the independent treasury, when finally established, did require exclusive specie payments to the government, it seems to follow that the administration favored such a policy from the beginning.

The second and related assumption originated with the argument that requiring specie payments would constitute the greatest governmental regulation of banks and therefore be anti-bank in nature. Benton's opposition to banks and enthusiasm for specie had linked the two together in the public mind, so that to champion specie was to attack banks. More realistically, there were some fears that the government's insistence upon specie payments would injure the banking inter-

42. Calhoun to James Calhoun, Sept. 7, 1837, April 18, 21, 1838, in Jameson, "Correspondence of John C. Calhoun," 377–379, 395.

est by forcing Jacksonians to implement the same procedures on the state level. New York Governor Marcy, shaken by the administration's support for an independent treasury, asked one of Van Buren's advisors "if the men of Washington expected that I was to proclaim a *Divorce* between the government of the State and the banks and advocate the exclusive use of coin in state transactions." Assured that such was not the case, Marcy replied, "Who then shall shield us . . . from the wrath of the loco-focos?"[43]

Under the misconception that the administration meant to insist upon specie payments, there were various economic predictions about the effect this policy would have on state banks. Many feared that their lending activities would be curtailed by a continual drain of specie; on the other hand, the government would also discharge its obligations with specie, causing it to flow back into state bank vaults. But the argument persisted that the government, pledged to limiting federal expenses, would allow valuable specie to be locked up in the Treasury, thus making it unavailable as a source of credit.[44]

Amid such apprehensions many believed that it would make the independent treasury bill more palatable to its anticipated critics in Congress if the government would receive bank paper. Other historians have concluded that this alternative posed a serious dilemma for the administration: the Calhounites would insist upon a specie clause in return for their sup-

43. Marcy to Prosper Wetmore, Sept. 9, 1837, Marcy Papers. The Conservative *Madisonian* warned its readers: "But establish the Sub-Treasury system, and its friends and sponsors will, of course, carry it out in all its details through the various machinery of the state governments" (*Madisonian*, Nov. 10, 1837).

44. Silas Wright defended such an eventuality as a valuable check upon bank credit expansion (*Congressional Globe*, 25 Cong., 1 sess., 92).

port, but to include such a clause in the proposal would force the pro-bank Conservatives into the opposition. This analysis is misleading.[45] It assumes that exclusive specie payments represented the firmest anti-bank position as well as the most effective regulatory approach to state banking, but such was not the case. In reality, the original Treasury proposal recommended that the government receive the paper of state banks, not in order to mollify Conservatives but as a more effective means of regulating bank notes. The independent treasury bill was defeated in the Twenty-fifth Congress primarily because Whigs and Conservative Democrats opposed an independent treasury in any form, but also because they recognized that the Treasury's acceptance of bank notes promised even more forceful regulation of state banks than did specie payments.

A detailed account of congressional consideration of the independent treasury proposal is necessary to support the above conclusions. The special session of Congress, called by Van Buren for September 1837, was not surprised by his recommendation of an independent treasury, since the *Globe* had already announced the government's intentions.[46] Most congressmen were unprepared, however, for the manner in which the administration presented its plan. The Secretary of the Treasury's report emphasized that Congress must deal with two separate issues. The first was the Treasury recommendation that federal funds be withdrawn from state banks and in the future be handled by government receivers; the second issue concerned the means of payment to the government. Contrary to predictions, Woodbury recommended that upon resumption of specie payments, the Treasury direct govern-

45. Sellers, *James K. Polk, Jacksonian.* For a somewhat different analysis of the administration's strategy on the independent treasury see Curtis, *The Fox at Bay*, chs. 4–7.
46. Washington *Globe*, July 7, 21, 1837.

ment receivers to accept state bank notes of local institutions and return them periodically for specie.[47] Silas Wright, whose responsibility it was to guide the bill through the Senate, revealed the administration's strategy to a fellow senator: it seemed obvious that the bill would be easier to get through Congress without the requirement of specie payments. Until the banks resumed specie payments the government could take only specie anyway; when the banks resumed specie payments, Woodbury would instruct his receivers to take the local bank notes and return them weekly for specie.[48]

Woodbury's proposal implied direct governmental regulation of the note issues of state banks. Such an implication was not surprising, radical, or unexpected to anyone familiar with Treasury operations during the pet banking era. The secretary, who had consistently but ineffectively labored to turn the pet bank system into a means of specie redemption to insure the value of bank notes, was now proposing more direct regulation by government. He was fully conscious of the expanded responsibilities such an independent treasury operation would mean for the Treasury itself. In his report to the special session of Congress, Woodbury indicated that the government's accumulation of specie would allow the Treasury department to issue certificates based upon its holdings.[49] Silas Wright, in his later defense of the proposal, admitted that these certificates would go into circulation and constitute a national currency.[50] Woodbury's report had pointed to the desirability of "some paper medium of higher character and other than what now exists in private bills of exchange or notes of state banks." The government's intentions, or at least

47. *Register of Debates,* 25 Cong., 1 sess., Appendix.
48. Niles to Welles, Sept. 15, 1837, Welles Papers.
49. *Register of Debates,* 25 Cong., 1 sess., Appendix, 21–22.
50. *Ibid.,* 450–451.

opportunities, were not overlooked by the administration's critics. The Treasury's recommendations convinced Senator Rives that "the real design of some . . . is to make war upon, and finally destroy the State institutions." He went on to warn his Conservative ally, Governor Campbell, of the plans for "government paper money, which is to supersede and displace the state currencies."[51]

But the administration's plan was upset when Calhoun finessed the Democrats by offering an amendment to the independent treasury bill requiring the government to receive only gold and silver. It was difficult to oppose Calhoun's amendment and still claim to be in favor of hard money. Consequently, the specie payment provision was included and the Senate approved the measure by five votes. With the Calhoun amendment the Senate bill was later tabled in the House by a vote of 119 to 107.[52]

The bill was lost but the regular session was to convene shortly; in the meantime the administration could evaluate the House vote and prepare for the upcoming session. A study of the vote revealed that four Virginia Democrats followed Rives' leadership in opposing the bill, while New York Democrats remained almost solidly with the administration rather than follow Tallmadge. The most unexpected behavior came from the South Carolina delegation. Despite the fact that Calhoun supported the bill after the inclusion of his own specie clause, eight of the nine congressmen from his state voted against it.[53]

When the regular session of Congress convened in December 1837, the independent treasury was the main order of

51. Rives to Campbell, Oct. 31, 1837, Campbell Papers.
52. *Senate Journal*, 25 Cong., 1 sess., 50–51, 55; *House Journal*, 25 Cong., 1 sess., 195–197.
53. *Ibid.*

business. Silas Wright introduced the administration's bill in January, but it was significantly changed from the last session. The new bill included a clause calling for progressive specie payments over a six-year period; at the end of that time, the government would receive only specie. There was also a section allowing the Secretary of the Treasury to invest any government surplus over $4 million in state or national stocks. Wright's speech explained the administration's change of mind. Acknowledging that the method of payment to the government was a very controversial part of the bill, he stated that the specie clause was included this time because it had been made a part of the bill at the last session, though the administration preferred it as originally introduced. Wright himself believed that a law which gave the banks six years to convert to specie payments might be preferable to the original plan to present bank notes "for payment at short intervals and in large masses," but claimed that the administration would follow either plan.[54]

The section of the bill which provided for investment of a surplus was included to thwart those who might argue that the public money would accumulate in the Treasury. It represented one of the few occasions when administration spokesmen publicly recognized the need for a governmental stimulus to the economy rather than restraints on bank credit. Calhoun attacked this provision on the grounds that the government's function should be to pursue policies that would avoid a surplus, not set up the means to dispose of it. Again, the South Carolinian was instructing the Jacksonians in their own language. Good Democrats who were pledged to retrenchment and a frugal government found Calhoun's argument irresistible and the clause was eliminated from the bill.[55]

54. *Congressional Globe*, 25 Cong., 2 sess., 109–112, Appendix, 86.
55. *Ibid.*, 153; *Senate Journal*, 25 Cong., 2 sess., 197.

The first test of Senate strength on the independent treasury measure came on a motion by James Buchanan of Pennsylvania to postpone a vote until the next session of Congress. Both Buchanan and Felix Grundy of Tennessee had been instructed by their state legislatures to oppose an independent treasury bill, instructions both declared they would obey even though they personally approved of the bill. The move to postpone was defeated by a vote of twenty-nine to twenty-three and the administration was assured of having the votes to pass the bill through the Senate. The only Democrats voting with Buchanan and Grundy to postpone were the Conservatives: Rives, Tallmadge, Tipton and Ruggles. They were also the only Democrats to oppose the measure on final passage, with the exception of Robert Nicholas of Louisiana, who apparently voted against postponement in order to have the fate of the bill settled during that session.[56]

Senate passage of the bill was insured, but in order to increase the chances of approval in the House Alfred Cuthbert, a Georgia Democrat, moved to strike the specie clause. All the Whigs supported the motion, as did the five Democratic Conservatives, Nicholas, Rives, Ruggles, Tallmadge and Tipton. The motion only carried, however, when nine Democratic supporters of the bill joined the Whigs and Conservatives on this vote.[57]

The elimination of the specie clause from the Senate bill resulted in the prominent defection of Calhoun, who voted against final passage and denounced the bill as a fraud. But the lack of Calhoun's support was no great political loss. His vote was not necessary for Senate passage and the House vote in the preceding session showed that the South Carolinian had little influence on that body. Moreover, Calhoun's alienation

56. *Ibid.*, 276, 320.   57. *Ibid.*, 313–314.

from the Democratic cause was welcomed by powerful Jacksonians who disliked his self-appointed leadership on the independent treasury issue, and generally regarded him as a dangerous rival.[58]

The Senate bill without the specie clause passed by a vote of twenty-seven to twenty-five,[59] but all five Democratic Conservatives opposed the bill, which should have raised the question of whether Conservative objections did not go beyond the specie clause.

A similar independent treasury bill had been introduced in the House, this one with a specie clause. The House then had a choice of two bills, their own, or the one from the Senate without a specie clause. Before the House had a chance to debate the merits of either bill, a motion to table the Senate bill was made and carried by a vote of 106 to 98.[60] The *Globe* branded this a "sinister" move by the House opposition, claiming that twenty-two absent members would have voted in favor of the bill.[61]

The House did not vote on its own bill until June, three months later. On a motion to have it pass to a third reading, the bill was rejected 125 to 111.[62] Both votes in the House indicate that the administration had no chance of getting a bill through in that session because the Conservatives and the Whigs voting together constituted a clear majority. The Democratic vote reached 111 because two members who had voted along with the Whigs and Conservatives to table the Senate bill then voted with the administration. One

58. William Preston to Willie Mangum, March 28, 1838, *Papers of Mangum*, II, 516–517.

59. *Senate Journal*, 25 Cong., 2 sess., 320.

60. *House Journal*, 25 Cong., 2 sess., 679–680.

61. Washington *Globe*, March 27, 1838.

62. *House Journal*, 25 Cong., 2 sess., 1157–1159.

Congressman, Hiram Gray, voted with the majority so as to be able to move a reconsideration, and Samuel Sawyer of North Carolina, a Calhounite, voted to table the Senate bill and voted for the House bill because he preferred the specie clause. The administration also gained nineteen of the absentees whom the *Globe* had correctly identified as administration supporters on the vote to table the Senate bill. However, eight congressmen who voted for the Senate bill crossed over to vote against the House bill. When these eight Conservative "swing" votes and opponents of the independent treasury who also were absent on the vote to table the Senate bill were added to the other Whigs and Conservatives in the House, they constituted a sufficient majority to defeat any administration bill.

Under these circumstances, the vote of the Calhounites in the House was only secondary in determining the final outcome of the bill. In fact, Samuel Sawyer of North Carolina was the only Calhounite to follow his leader on these two votes. Every member from South Carolina voted against tabling the Senate bill, even though Calhoun had voted against it in the Senate and even branded it hypocritical. Dixon Lewis, the Alabama Calhounite, also voted not to table the Senate bill. In the vote on the House bill containing a specie clause, the Calhounites did vote with the administration. Robert Campbell and Hugh Legare, however, two congressmen from South Carolina who had voted against tabling the Senate bill, then voted against the House bill and added to the Conservative-Whig coalition in the House.

It was not the Calhoun faction, therefore, which defeated the independent treasury, but rather the Conservatives. Numerically, they were much stronger in the House than the Calhounites (the *Madisonian* identified eight members of the House as Calhounites while claiming at least sixteen members were Conservatives).[63] While it is true that a bill without the specie clause might have had a better chance in the House by attracting Conservative votes, it is unlikely that any such bill would have passed. Eight Conservatives voted against tabling the Senate bill, presumably on the grounds that if any bill were to be called up they preferred the one without the specie clause. But this was merely a vote not to table; it is doubtful if enough of them would have voted for final passage of any bill. One Conservative in this group, Henry Foster of New York, moved to reconsider the vote on the House bill for the purpose of eliminating the specie clause, thus making the bill acceptable to him. It was then pointed out that the vote on both bills showed there was enough Conservative strength against the bill in any form to constitute a majority with the Whigs. The Democratic leadership agreed and the vote to reconsider only attracted twenty-one votes: twenty administration supporters plus Foster.[64]

It is clear that Conservatives, at least as far as their opinions were represented by Rives, Tallmadge, and the *Madisonian* editors, were opposed to the independent treasury whether the government received the notes of specie-paying banks or not. Since, under the administration's plan, the government receivers would take the notes of local banks in their vicinity only to return them promptly for specie, the fact that the government would receive bank notes was of little consolation to Conservatives. "I cannot perceive any substantial difference between requiring gold and silver, in the first instance, in payment of public dues, and receiving bank notes only to be converted into gold and silver," Rives wrote to Governor Campbell.[65]

---

63. *Madisonian*, June 28, 30, 1838.
64. *Congressional Globe*, 25 Cong., 2 sess., 480.
65. Rives to Campbell, Feb. 6, 1838, Campbell Papers.

But Senator Tallmadge noted a difference and regarded the bill without the specie clause as a greater threat to state banks because it gave the Secretary of the Treasury direct power over their note issues. When the Senate passed an independent treasury bill without the specie clause, the *Madisonian* attacked the bill as giving the government "unlimited control over the currency of the country."[66] This kind of direct governmental control over state bank note issues was precisely the Conservatives' fundamental objection to the independent treasury. They wanted the government to receive the notes of state banks, but only if they were redeposited in selected state banks and credited to the government as cash. This would have placed upon the banking system itself the primary responsibility for settling balances between the government and the banks. Tallmadge wrote to Rives when the plan for an independent treasury was first proposed, "I am opposed to the Government thus directly interfering in these matters."[67]

Democratic attitudes toward banks had come full circle. The Jacksonian crusade had started in 1829 with an ambiguous attack on banking which found clarity and a vulnerable target in the "Monster" BUS of Philadelphia. Subsequently forced to ally with the "money power" during the pet banking era, Democrats, after the banking suspension, were on more comfortable and familiar ground in denouncing all banking connections with the government as intrinsically corrupting. Administration Democrats were eager to confess the sin of trusting banks in the first place. All mistakes, folly, avarice, and corruption which were laid at the doors of state banks and once indignantly denied by loyal Democrats during the heyday of pet banking were later enthusiastically embraced by the same Democrats as proof of the unreliability of banks

66. *Madisonian*, March 27, 1838.
67. Tallmadge to Rives, May 31, 1837, Rives Papers.

and the necessity for government to separate its affairs from them.[68] Democrats were understandably more anti-banking after the Panic of 1837 than before, though the administration's leaders defended the independent treasury proposal as actually being in the interest of banking as well as that of the public.

It was this theme of public responsibility which mitigated Democratic moralism on banking. Influential, and by then experienced, Jacksonians had come to realize the importance of some centralized controls over state bank notes, the most prevalent form of bank credit. Silas Wright made exactly this point in Senate debate on the independent treasury while reminding Whig opponents of the bill that they had consistently termed the restraints of a national bank on state bank issues "salutary and proper." Wright pointed out that an independent treasury would "form the same check and restraint upon the local banking institutions . . . How then is it possible that those who saw such benign influences to the local institutions from the wholesome restraints of a national bank, should see such baneful effects to follow the same influences, when flowing from the public Treasury?"[69]

An independent treasury, however, was not the Jacksonian surrogate for a central bank. The various administration-sponsored recommendations in Congress emphasized the restrictive side of central banking while denying any governmental responsibility for augmenting bank credit. Woodbury's recommendation that the Treasury issue certificates

68. Webster's post-Panic call to investigate the Democratic-controlled Commonwealth Bank of Boston was supported by Senator Niles on the grounds that it would "prove the necessity of disconnecting the Treasury from all banks" (Niles to Welles, Jan. 17, 1838, Welles Papers).

69. *Congressional Globe*, 25 Cong., 2 sess., Appendix, 91.

based upon government holdings of specie represented a return to Jacksonian economic fundamentalism, rather than a recognition of the need for central banking. He made the rather startling statement to Congress that the problem with banking was that "a wide departure has been made from the original principles of having its issues of paper rest on a foundation consisting of specie alone."[70] However, it is not surprising that having experienced two periods of speculative inflation, both resulting in the collapse of the banking structure, Jacksonians would concentrate their attention on restricting credit expansion, believing as they did that the banking community needed responsible restraints rather than artificial stimulation.

70. *Ibid.*, 12. Kendall reportedly shared these views; Governor Marcy wrote to a friend in the summer of 1837: "I was told by a person who had conversed with Mr. Kendall that he was for restricting bank circulation to the actual amount of specie deposited in the bank" (Marcy to P. Wetmore, Aug. 18, 1837, Marcy Papers).

8

Conclusion

This study has focused on the Jacksonian political response to the economic expansion of the 1830's, concentrating particularly on the inner circle of Jacksonians involved in determining the federal government's responsibility for state banking. Rather than dealing with mass electorate behavior or the allegiances of bankers, manufacturers, planters and other groups, it has been written, so to speak, from the inside out.

The historiographical context is the conflict between Arthur Schlesinger's anti-business conclusions regarding Jacksonian Democracy and Bray Hammond's version of the Jacksonians as incipient entrepreneurs, the latter theory being judged unpersuasive here. The fact that there were petty entrepreneurial bankers, wealthy speculators, and bogus workingmen among the Jacksonian cadre should surprise no one familiar with the workings of American politics. But the argument that a causal connection exists between their interests and overall Jacksonian policy is seriously misleading. We have seen, for example, how state bankers operating under governmental regulations in the aftermath of the Bank War were, if anything, cautiously hostile to Democratic policy.

Furthermore, the Jackson administration's pet banking

operation as it was originally established was not a design for orgies of speculation and laissez-faire rapaciousness; it was an effort to keep the decaying "Monster" BUS at bay with one hand while awkwardly attempting to satisfy society's needs with the other. Later, when the functions of pet banking were more stable, Jacksonians attempted to impose regulatory controls upon banking and still remain true to their anti-centralization, pro-states rights political creed. Finally, the Van Buren proposal for an independent treasury became the last effort by the Jacksonians to fuse some governmental control of banking with their commitment to decentralization. That they did not succeed in these efforts is obvious, but it is a mistake to interpret their failures as conscious, premeditated policy.

The anti-entrepreneurial conclusions drawn throughout this study may seem to portray Jacksonians as disinterested guardians of the public welfare, dealing forcefully with economic excesses; but merely standing the entrepreneurial thesis on its head in such a way must be avoided. A basic fault of both the anti-business and pro-business approach to Jacksonian Democracy has been to concentrate on economics and interest group motives. The present analysis has argued that economic interests were subordinated to political interests.

The significant event during the Jacksonian era was not the triumph of laissez faire or a protoregulatory state but the emergence and establishment of a new political party system. The older political arrangements were democratized, and the political process became unpredictable and difficult to manage. Economic pressure groups, political opportunists, and others maneuvered within the new organizations for leverage on the party machinery. The diversity of the new political system posed a formidable task for those who were responsible for providing some legitimacy for organized political affiliation. Under such circumstances the political moralizers gained access to the decision-making process, to a much greater degree than either the banking interest or any combination of economic interests. These were the insiders who made political decisions and then justified them on abstract ideological grounds. In making their decisions, however, the new political managers were sensitive to a variety of preconceptions and social forces which permeated the American experience.

There was a peculiar dichotomy at the center of American life which influenced political action: it consisted of believing in a homogeneous society and at the same time fearing that alien or subversive forces might undermine the good society.[1] Jacksonians and Whigs alike were alarmed at the ease with which their fellow Americans could be lured away from loyalty to basic principles. The remedy was to be constantly on guard, lest liberty and freedom be lost. Consciously or unconsciously, Jacksonians were superbly successful at politicizing such fears in their anti-bank crusade. They were masters at anti-bank rhetoric aimed at stimulating political awareness and energizing the public into a sense of duty and responsibility, but when the wars were won they were often confused and disoriented in the aftermath of the victory.

---

1. This insight into the American political character, as well as many others, was first explored by Richard Hofstader. See especially Hofstader's *The Paranoid Style in American Politics and Other Essays* (New York, 1966); also David Brion Davis, "Some Themes of Counter Subversion: An Analysis of Anti-Masonic, Anti-Catholic, and Anti-Mormon Literature," *Mississippi Valley Historical Review*, XLVII (Sept. 1960), 205–224. John R. Howe, Jr., *The Changing Political Thought of John Adams* (Princeton, 1966) is an exceptionally fine study of the theme that moral lassitude threatened the promise of the virtuous American Republic in the eyes of one of its founders.

Jacksonians were more interested in denouncing banks than in regulating them.

Another influence on American political life was the dramatization of the money issue into a moral event. This theme has been brilliantly stated in Marvin Meyers' study of the Jacksonian personality and argued persuasively by Irwin Unger and Walter T. K. Nugent in their respective studies of post-Civil War financial and political problems.[2] What these works show (and this analysis supports) is that the money question forced various groups to re-examine their self-images. Marvin Meyers has demonstrated that many Jacksonians engaged in a moral crusade which touched deeply felt anxieties, suspicions, and fears among the populace. Irwin Unger, in his study of Reconstruction finance, argues that the firm hold of moral values upon most Americans in the nineteenth century should be recognized by historians. While admitting the lack of a statistical balance sheet for evaluating moral suasion, he contends that it was more important than the economic motives stressed by Progressive historians. As Unger puts it, "Political man often subdued economic man in the struggle over money." Nugent agrees, and in his study of late nineteenth century finance argues that the "money question" presented Americans with choices which could not be compromised: "Money was critical because it was moral," he concludes.[3]

The issue of money in nineteenth century America perpetrated a moral exchange between members of society about the meaning of life. In the Jacksonian era this conflict was

2. Marvin Meyers, *The Jacksonian Persuasion: Politics and Belief* (Stanford, 1957); Irwin Unger, *The Greenback Era: A Social and Political History of American Finance, 1865–1879* (Princeton, 1964); Walter T. K. Nugent, *Money and American Society, 1865–1880* (New York, 1968).
3. Meyers, ch. 2; Unger, 7–8, 25; Nugent, 273–275.

politicized and the ensuing political rhetoric became a vital force in itself. Jacksonians, more than Whigs, were drawn to the new political moralism, sensing that the quickened tempo of economic change somehow violated Calvinist loyalties to hard work, thrift and duty. If this exhausted the Jacksonian response to the expanded economic opportunities, it would be interesting only as an example of political opportunism or quixotic crusading; but it has been shown in the preceding pages that even as the Jacksonians articulated their moralistic position on banking, they were compelled to act politically in ways which often threatened the stability of the coalition they had so artfully constructed.

But why were Jacksonians more influenced by moralism than Whigs? The answer is that they were not; the two parties simply disagreed on which issues properly should be considered moral and which political. It should be emphasized that Jacksonians moralized those issues regarded as distinctly political—the "Monster" Bank and hard money, for example. By contrast, the Whigs may have been pragmatists about such economic issues but they often attempted to introduce into the political arena other issues, such as religion, prohibition, alien voting rights (and later slavery) which appeared to many to be apolitical in nature. The Jacksonian response was to regard such issues as distinctly moral rather than legislative and to dismiss them as threats to the traditional separation between church and state.[4] One may sum it up this way: The

4. On the Whig attraction for the morally coercive power of government see Ronald P. Formisano, "Political Character, Antipartyism and the Second American Party System," *American Quarterly* (Winter 1969), 683–709. The Jacksonian opposition to those who petitioned against Sunday mail deliveries on the grounds that it violated the separation between church and state is well known; less well known is the fact that Jacksonians continued to use this theme against those who petitioned Congress to abolish slavery in the Dis-

Jacksonians preferred to moralize politics while the Whigs attempted to politicize morality.

The moral dimensions of the money issue and its political complications determined the Jacksonian management of pet banking operations. As Secretary of the Treasury, Levi Woodbury was no ideological automaton; his expedient policies represented a preference neither for laissez faire nor iron-clad bank regulation. He was a rather colorless, unimaginative administrator, concerned, as are most men in public life, with his own reputation and political future. Concerned also with his responsibility for the public money, Woodbury attempted to function as a loyal Jacksonian while cooperating with powerful bankers, but his efforts were defeated by the tensions inherent in any alliance between Jacksonianism and the "money power."

In belatedly recognizing the need for some centralized banking restraints, Jacksonians like Woodbury were forced to consider the uncomfortable alternatives of direct governmental regulation or a national bank. Rather than choose more direct control, they gravitated toward the free flow of specie as a natural regulator of economic affairs. Thus the Jacksonians' preference for specie was more than economic primitivism; it satisfied their search for an impersonal regulator of the volatile American economy. Moreover, since economic controls are more acceptable when they appear to emanate from a disinterested mechanism, the Jacksonians elevated specie to the level of a financial *deus ex machina*.

The Jacksonian fetish for specie, coupled with the expanding anti-bank mood, led many Democrats into the peculiar

---

trict of Columbia. Churchill Cambreleng argued that the abolitionists "are our most bitter opponents. They are, almost exclusively the old 'Church and State' faction which has been annually petitioning about Sunday Mails" (Washington *Globe*, Feb. 13, 1836).

position of supporting rather advanced banking regulation. It was essential to the conscience of the Jacksonian that his position on specie be interpreted as an anti-bank stand rather than an admission of the necessity for banking regulation, though it all worked to the same end; hard-money rhetoric served as a verbal camouflage for the regulations Woodbury imposed upon the pet banks. By 1836 it was clear that the uneasy alliance between those Democrats who were against all banks and those who advocated Treasury regulation through the Wall Street pets could no longer sustain itself against increasing demands for an inflated money market and a more definite separation from banks. After the financial "infidelity" of bankers was exposed by their suspension of specie payments in 1837, the next step—divorce—was inevitable.

Selected Bibliography

Manuscripts

Nicholas Biddle Papers. Microfilm. University of California, Berkeley.

David Campbell Papers. Microfilm. Wisconsin State Historical Society.

Andrew Jackson Donelson Papers. Library of Congress.

Thomas Ewing Papers. Library of Congress.

Azariah C. Flagg Papers. New York Public Library.

Andrew Jackson Papers. Microfilm. University of California, Berkeley.

Lewis-Neilson Papers. Historical Society of Pennsylvania.

William Marcy Papers. Library of Congress.

George Newbold Papers. New-York Historical Society.

Nathaniel Niles Papers. Library of Congress.

David Perine Papers. Maryland Historical Society.

James K. Polk Papers. Microfilm. University of California, Berkeley.

William C. Rives Papers. Library of Congress.

Andrew Stevenson Papers. Library of Congress.

Roger B. Taney Papers. Library of Congress.

United States Treasury Papers. Letters to Banks, Letters from Banks, Recommendations of Banks, Letters from Mint. National Archives.

Martin Van Buren Papers. Microfilm. University of California, Berkeley.

Gideon Welles Papers. Library of Congress.

Levi Woodbury Papers. Library of Congress.

Printed Correspondence and Personal Memoirs

Bassett, John S., ed. *The Correspondence of Andrew Jackson.* 7 vols. Washington, 1926–1935.

Benton, Thomas H. *Thirty Years' View; or, a History of the Working of the American Government for Thirty Years, from 1820 to 1850.* 2 vols. New York, 1854–1856.

Bruchey, Stuart, ed. "Roger Brooke Taney's Account of His Relations with Thomas Ellicott in the Bank War," *Maryland Historical Magazine*, LIII (March, June 1958), 58–74, 131–152.

Duane, William J. *Narrative and Correspondence Concerning the Removal of the Deposits and Occurrences Connected Therewith.* Philadelphia, 1838.

Hamilton, James A. *Reminiscences of James A. Hamilton.* New York, 1869.

Hammond, Jabez D. *The History of Political Parties in the State of New York.* 2 vols. Albany, 1842.

Jameson, J. Franklin, ed. "Correspondence of John C. Calhoun," *Annual Report of the American Historical Association for the Year 1899.* Vol. II. Washington, 1900.

Kendall, Amos. *Autobiography of Amos Kendall.* Boston, 1872.

McGrane, Reginald C., ed. *The Correspondence of Nicholas Biddle Dealing with National Affairs, 1807–1844.* Boston, 1919.

Robertson, Nellie A., and Dorothy Riker, eds. *The John Tipton Papers.* 3 vols. Indianapolis, 1942.

Shanks, Henry T., ed. *The Papers of Willie Person Mangum.* 4 vols. Raleigh, N.C., 1950–1955.

Van Buren, Martin. "The Autobiography of Martin Van Buren," ed. John C. Fitzpatrick, *Annual Report of the American Historical Association for the Year 1918.* Vol. II. Washington, 1920.

Secondary Works

Alexander, Thomas B. *Sectional Stress and Party Strength: A Study of Roll Call Voting Patterns in the United States House of Representatives, 1836–1860.* Nashville, 1967.

Ammon, Harry. "The Richmond Junto, 1800–1824," *Virginia Magazine of History and Biography*, LXI (1953), 395–418.

Benson, Lee. *The Concept of Jacksonian Democracy: New York as a Test Case.* Princeton, 1961.

Braverman, Howard. "The Economic and Political Background of the Conservative Revolt in Virginia," *Virginia Magazine of History and Biography*, LX (1952), 266–287.

Brown, Richard H. "The Missouri Crisis, Slavery, and the Politics of Jacksonianism," *South Atlantic Quarterly*, LXV (Winter 1966), 55–72.

Bryan, Alfred C. *History of State Banking in Maryland.* Johns Hopkins University Studies in Historical and Political Science, XVII. Baltimore, 1899.

Buley, R. C. *The Old Northwest Pioneer Period, 1815–1840.* 2 vols. Indianapolis 1950.

Catteral, Ralph C. H. *The Second Bank of the United States.* Chicago, 1903.

Cave, Alfred. *Jacksonian Democracy and the Historians.* Gainesville, Fla., 1964.

Chaddock, Robert E. *The Safety Fund Banking System in New York, 1829–1866.* Washington, 1910.

Chambers, William N. *Old Bullion Benton, Senator from the New West.* Boston, 1956.

Chase, James S. "Jacksonian Democracy and the Rise of the Nominating Convention, *Mid America*, XLV (Oct. 1963), 229–249.

Cole, Donald B. *Jacksonian Democracy in New Hampshire, 1800–1851.* Cambridge, Mass., 1970.

Curtis, James C. *The Fox at Bay: Martin Van Buren and the Presidency, 1837–1841.* Lexington, Ky., 1970.

Darling, Arthur B. *Political Change in Massachusetts, 1824–1848.* New Haven, 1925.

Degler, Carl N. "The Loco focos: Urban Agrarians," *Journal of Economic History*, XVI (Sept. 1956), 322–333.

Dewey, Davis R. *State Banking before the Civil War*. Washington, 1910.

Donovan, Herbert D. A. *The Barnburners: A Study of the Internal Movements in the Political History of New York State*. New York, 1925.

Dorfman, Joseph. *The Economic Mind in American Civilization, 1606–1918*. 3 vols. New York, 1946–1949.

——. "The Jackson Wage Earner Thesis," *American Historical Review*, LIV (Jan. 1947), 296–306.

Garraty, John A. *Silas Wright*. New York, 1949.

Gatell, Frank Otto. "Money and Party in Jacksonian America: A Quantitative Look at New York's Men of Quality," *Political Science Quarterly*, LXXXII (June 1967), 235–252.

——. "Secretary Taney and the Baltimore Pets: A Study in Banking and Politics," *Business History Review*, XXXIX (Spring 1965), 205–227.

——. "Sober Second Thoughts on Van Buren, The Albany Regency, and the Wall Street Conspiracy," *Journal of American History*, LIII (June 1966), 19–40.

——. "Spoils of the Bank War: Political Bias in the Selection of Pet Banks," *American Historical Review*, LXX (Oct. 1964), 35–58.

Govan, Thomas P. *Nicholas Biddle: Nationalist and Public Banker, 1786–1844*. Chicago, 1959.

Haller, Mark H. "The Rise of the Jackson Party in Maryland, 1820–1829," *Journal of Southern History*, XXVIII (Aug. 1962), 307–326.

Hammond, Bray. *Banks and Politics in America from the Revolution to the Civil War*. Princeton, 1957.

Harrison, Joseph H., Jr. "Martin Van Buren and His Southern Supporters," *Journal of Southern History*, XXII (Nov. 1956), 438–450.

Hasse, William F., Jr. *A History of Banking in New Haven, Connecticut*. New Haven, 1946.

Heath, Milton S. *Constructive Liberalism: The Role of the State in Economic Development in Georgia to 1860.* Cambridge, Mass., 1954.

Hoffman, William S. *Andrew Jackson and North Carolina Politics.* Chapel Hill, N.C., 1958.

Hofstader, Richard. *The American Political Tradition and the Men Who Made It.* New York, 1957.

Hugins, Walter. *Jacksonian Democracy and the Working Class: A Study Of the New York Workingmen's Movement, 1829–1837.* Stanford, 1960.

Huntington, Charles C. *A History of Banking and Currency in Ohio before the Civil War.* Columbus, 1915.

Kinley, David. *The Independent Treasury of the United States.* Washington, 1910.

Lebowitz, Michael A. "The Jacksonians: Paradox Lost?" in Barton J. Bernstein, ed., *Towards a New Past: Dissenting Essays in American History.* New York, 1968.

Lively, Robert. "The American System: A Review Article," *Business History Review,* XXIX (March 1955), 81–96.

McCormick, Richard P. "New Perspectives on Jacksonian Politics," *American Historical Review,* LXV (Jan. 1960), 288–301.

——. *The Second American Party System: Party Formation in the Jacksonian Era.* Chapel Hill, N.C., 1966.

Macesich, George. "Sources of Monetary Disturbances in the United States, 1834–1845," *Journal of Economic History,* XX (Sept. 1960), 407–434.

Madeline, Sister M. Grace, *Monetary and Banking Theories of Jacksonian Democracy.* Philadelphia, 1943.

Marshall, Lynn. "The Strange Stillbirth of the Whig Party," *American Historical Review,* LXXII (Jan. 1967), 445–468.

Mering, John V. *The Whig Party in Missouri.* Columbia, Mo., 1967.

Meyers, Marvin. *The Jacksonian Persuasion: Politics and Belief.* Stanford, 1957.

Miles, Edward A. *Jacksonian Democracy in Mississippi.* Chapel Hill, N.C., 1960.

Miller, Harry E. *Banking Theories in the United States before 1860.* Cambridge, Mass., 1927.

Miller, Nathan. *The Enterprise of a Free People: Aspects of Economic Development in New York State during the Canal Period, 1792–1838.* Ithaca, N.Y., 1962.

Morse, Jarvis M. *A Neglected Period of Connecticut's History: 1818–1850.* New Haven, 1933.

Pease, Theodore C. *The Frontier State, 1818–1840: The Centennial History of Illinois.* Vol 2. Chicago, 1919.

Pessen, Edward. *Jacksonian America Society, Personality, and Politics.* Homewood, Ill., 1969.

Redlich, Fritz. *The Molding of American Banking: Men and Ideas.* 2 vols. New York, 1947, 1951.

Remini, Robert V. *Andrew Jackson and the Bank War.* New York, 1967.

——. *The Election of Andrew Jackson.* Philadelphia, 1963.

——. *Martin Van Buren and the Making of the Democratic Party.* New York, 1959.

Scheiber, Harry N. "George Bancroft and the Bank of Michigan, 1837–1841," *Michigan History,* XLIV (March 1960), 82–90.

——. "The Pet Banks in Jacksonian Politics and Finance, 1833–1841," *Journal of Economic History,* XXIII (June 1963), 196–214.

Schlesinger, Arthur M., Jr. *The Age of Jackson.* Boston, 1945.

Sellers, Charles G. *James K. Polk, Jacksonian, 1795–1843.* Princeton, 1957.

——. "Andrew Jackson versus the Historians," *Mississippi Valley Historical Review,* XLIV (March 1958), 615–634.

——. "Banking and Politics in Jackson's Tennessee, 1817–1827," *Mississippi Valley Historical Review,* XLI (June 1954), 61–84.

Sharp, James Roger. *The Jacksonians versus the Banks Politics in the States after the Panic of 1837.* New York, 1970.

Simms, H. H. *The Rise of the Whigs in Virginia, 1824–1840.* Richmond, Va., 1929.

Smith, Elbert B. *Magnificent Missourian: The Life of Thomas Hart Benton.* Philadelphia, 1958.

Smith, Walter B. *Economic Aspects of the Second Bank of the United States.* Cambridge, 1953.

Smith, William E. *The Francis Preston Blair Family in Politics.* 2 vols. New York, 1933.

Snyder, Charles M. *The Jacksonian Heritage: Pennsylvania Politics, 1833–1848.* Harrisburg, Pa., 1958.

Spencer, Ivor D. *The Victor and the Spoils: A Life of William L. Marcy.* Providence, 1959.

Starnes, George T. *Sixty Years of Branch Banking in Virginia.* New York, 1931.

Stevens, Harry R. *The Early Jacksonian Party in Ohio.* Durham, N.C., 1957.

Swisher, Carl B. *Roger B. Taney.* New York, 1935.

Taus, Esther R. *Central Banking Functions of the United States Treasury, 1789–1941.* New York, 1943.

Taylor, George R. *The Transportation Revolution, 1815–1860.* New York, 1951.

Temin, Peter. *The Jacksonian Economy.* New York, 1969.

Thompson, Charles M. "The Illinois Whigs before 1846," *University of Illinois Studies in the Social Sciences,* IV. Urbana, 1915.

Timberlake, Richard H., Jr. "The Specie Circular and Distribution of the Surplus," *Journal of Political Economy,* LXVIII (April 1960), 109–117.

——. "The Specie Standard and Central Banking in the United States before 1860," *Journal of Economic History,* XXI (Sept. 1961), 318–341.

Trimble, William. "Diverging Tendencies in New York Democracy in the Period of the Loco focos," *American Historical Review,* XXIV (April 1919), 396–421.

Van Deusen, Glyndon G. *The Jacksonian Era, 1828–1848.* New York, 1959.

——. "Some Aspects of Whig Thought and Theory in the Jacksonian Period," *American Historical Review,* LXIII (Jan. 1958), 305–322.

Van Fenstermaker, Joseph. *The Development of American Commercial Banking, 1782–1837.* Kent, Ohio, 1965.

Ward, John W. *Andrew Jackson: Symbol for an Age.* New York, 1955.

White, Leonard D. *The Jacksonians: A Study in Administrative History, 1829–1861.* New York, 1954.

Wilburn, Jean Alexander. *Biddle's Bank: The Crucial Years.* New York, 1967.

Wiltse, Charles M. *John C. Calhoun, Nullifier, 1829–1839.* Indianapolis, 1949.

Index

The Politics of
Jacksonian Finance

Designed by R. E. Rosenbaum.
Composed by Kingsport Press, Inc.
in 11 point linotype Janson, 3 points leaded,
with display lines in monotype Janson.
Printed letterpress from type by Kingsport Press
on Warren's Number 66 text, 60 pound basis,
with the Cornell University Press watermark.
Bound by Kingsport Press.

Library of Congress Cataloging in Publication Data
(For library cataloging purposes only)

McFaul, John M   .
  The politics of Jacksonian finance.

  Bibliography:
    1. Banks and banking—United States—History.
    2. Currency question—United States—History.
    3. United States—Politics and government—1815–1861.
I. Title.
HG2471.M3   332.1'0973   72–4635
ISBN 0–8014–0738–9